Improving Tourism and Hospitality Services

Improving Tourism and Hospitality Services

Eric Laws

CABI Publishing

CABI Publishing is a division of CAB International

CABI Publishing
CAB International
Wallingford
Oxon OX10 8DE
UK

Tel: +44 (0)1491 832111
Fax: +44 (0)1491 833508
E-mail: cabi@cabi.org
Website: www.cabi-publishing.org

CABI Publishing
875 Massachusetts Avenue
7th Floor
Cambridge, MA 02139
USA

Tel: +1 617 395 4056
Fax: +1 617 354 6875
E-mail: cabi-nao@cabi.org

A catalogue record for this book is available from the British Library,
London, UK.
A catalogue record for this book is available from the Library of Congress,
Washington, DC, USA.

ISBN 0 85199 995 6

Typeset by Kenneth Burnley, Wirral, Cheshire, and Columns Design Ltd,
Reading, UK.
Printed and bound in the UK by Biddles Ltd, King's Lynn.

Contents

Figures   ix
Tables   xi
Case studies   xiii
Acknowledgements   xiv
Introduction   xv

Chapter 1   Service quality in tourism and hospitality
Introduction   1
The context to contemporary tourism service provision   2
Tourism and hospitality service failures   4
Case studies   6
Analysing tourism service quality   9
Conclusion   11

Chapter 2   Tourism and hospitality service quality research
Introduction   13
The distinguishing characteristics of tourism services   16
The challenge of managing services   19
Myopia in managing services   20
Service encounters – moments of truth   22
Theoretical frameworks for tourism and hospitality service
    research   22
Qualitative research and case studies   28
Case studies of service problems   28
Conclusion   30

Chapter 3 Analysing service experiences in tourism and hospitality

Introduction	32
Events in tourists' experiences	32
Satisfaction boosters and depressants	36
Service phases, episodes and events	37
Consumerist gap taxonomy for service encounter analysis	38
Consumerist gap research methods	38
The diary method and its limitations	40
Just noticeable differences	40
Content analysis theory	41
Critical incident techniques	42
Expectations of responses to service difficulties	43
A synthesis of service experiences and service design	46
Conclusion	46

Chapter 4 Tourism and hospitality service delivery systems

Introduction	48
Technical aspects of service systems	48
Style considerations	50
Performance criteria	54
Design errors	55
Service blueprinting	57
Mapping tourism services	60
Development of service blueprinting	61
Service blueprinting as a research tool	62
Perceptual blueprinting	72
Implications for organizational change	73
Conclusion	77

Chapter 5 Service quality and tourist satisfaction

Introduction	79
Definitions of quality	79
Issues in service quality	80
Gaps between expectations and service experiences	85
SERVQUAL	85
SERVQUAL and tourism	87
The SERVQUAL debate	89
Dissatisfaction with services	90

The costs of managing service quality 91
Conclusion 99

Chapter 6   Marketing tourism and hospitality services
Introduction 100
The service marketing paradigm 100
The significance of influencing consumer choice 101
Core and enhanced services 103
Service bundles 106
Differentiating tourism services 108
Positioning tourism services 109
Exaggerated service claims 112
Issues in pricing tourism services 115
Pricing inclusive holidays 116
Seasonal pricing 117
Late booking 118
Responses to late offers 119
Price relativities as a signal of product quality 120
Reducing price levels and broadening market demand 122
Customer loyalty 122
Further consideration of tourism purchasing decisions:
    consumer involvement 123
Time in the experience of tourist services 126
Conclusion 129

Chapter 7   Improving tourism and hospitality service systems
Introduction 130
Service management 131
Dyadic and multiplex service interactions 133
Customer participation in services 134
Service encounters 135
Service performance: further discussion 139
The Servuction approach 140
Quality control 141
Service standards 141
Quality control in tourism services 142
ISO 9000 143
Quality audits 144
Profit impacts of service quality control measures 145
Service problem or service crisis? 146

Learning from complaints 147
Service interruptions 148
Understanding passenger expectations during delay
    management 150
The costs of quality control 155
Conclusion 157

**Chapter 8 The management of tourism and hospitality
organizations**
Introduction 158
First or second generation service thinking 158
Managing service companies 160
Organizational climate 162
Service design and organizational cultures 167
Interdependency in the holiday industry 170
The limits of management control 173
Further considerations 176
Conclusion 177

Appendix: slides for a management development workshop 178
Bibliography 183
Index 201

Figures

2.1	The factors contributing to tourists' satisfaction	15
2.2	The tourism industry system	24
2.3	Development pressures on service design	30
3.1	Sequence of events in a journey	33
3.2	The consumerist gap	34
3.3	Satisfaction outcomes of contrasting responses to similar problems	44
3.4	Response profiles to service problems	46
3.5	Grid analysis of consumerist gap outcomes	47
4.1	Basic restaurant service blueprint	59
4.2	The nine cells of a full blueprint	62
4.3	The pizza restaurant blueprint	65
4.4	The pizza delivery blueprint	69
4.5	Perceptual map of an inclusive holiday	74
4.6	Managerial planning for an inclusive holiday	76
5.1	SERVQUAL: a tourism application	88
5.2	Conceptual blueprint of visitor management at Leeds Castle	98
6.1	Marketing core and enhanced services	105
6.2	Service positioning map	111
6.3	Effects on satisfaction of exaggerated advertising claims	113
6.4	A general model of seasonal price banding	118
6.5	Tourist consequences of differing price/quality combinations	121
6.6	A market clearing model	127
6.7	Service consumption model	128
7.1	Routes for passengers and staff through airport processes: complexity and repetition	137

7.2   Satisfaction management during a delay   154
8.1   Concepts of service organizations   161
8.2   The triangle of service   161

Tables

1.1 The main complaints from hotel guests 6
2.1 Differences between manufacturing and services 16
2.2 Contrasted management challenges in manufacturing and services 20
2.3 Complaints and compliments to an airline during one month 29
3.1 Consumerist gap acid test of flights 36
3.2 Journeys by air: phases and events 37
3.3 Consumerist gap taxonomy for service encounter analysis 39
4.1 Non-economic regulations on airlines 50
4.2 Factors to consider when developing the physical layout of a service 54
4.3 Effective performance targets 54
4.4 Pizza delivery service analysis 70
5.1 Passenger perceptions of airline service quality 84
5.2 General service gaps 86
5.3 Satisfaction diary of a visit to Leeds Castle 94
5.4 Visitor satisfaction management at Leeds Castle 96
6.1 Tourist choice and risk 102
6.2 Customer flows 103
6.3 Service innovation and competition 106
6.4 Tourism service development and service innovation 107
6.5 Differentiating tourism services 108
6.6 Impacts for Canterbury's stakeholders 114
6.7 Consumer involvement and choice between brands 126
7.1 Steps in managing services 131
7.2 Interactions during services 133
7.3 Difficulties in dealing with customers 134

7.4	Service encounters	138
7.5	Issues in tourism quality standards	141
7.6	ISO service elements	144
7.7	Features of museum service quality	145
7.8	Sources of dissatisfaction during a long delay	152
7.9	Costs of quality management	156
8.1	Key aspects of managerial roles	166
8.2	Excellent service management	168
8.3	Role of the CEO in implementing customer orientation	168
8.4	Corporate culture	169
8.5	Interdependencies in the tourism industry	172
8.6	Management control of factors affecting customer satisfaction	175

Case Studies

1.1   The Edinburgh Airport buses   7
2.1   The variability of tourists' service experiences   17
3.1   Contrasting flight experiences: non-availability of vegetarian meals   43
4.1   Constraints to airline services   49
4.2   Service differentiation through cabin design   52
4.3   A new ticket hall   55
4.4   Managing tourists' activities in China   56
4.5   Blueprinting analysis of a pizza restaurant and delivery service   63
5.1   Managing visits to castles   92
6.1   Positioning hotels in Port Douglas, Tropical North Queensland   110
7.1   A long flight delay   151
8.1   Changing the management style at British Airways   163

Acknowledgements

I wish to thank the many tourism managers who have discussed their experiences with me during my career and who thereby provided the foundations and the inspiration for this book. Among the many other tourism enthusiasts to whom I express my gratitude are my students and colleagues, who have shared with me their thoughts on many of the ideas presented here. Professors Gary Akehurst, Stephen Wanhill and Chris Cooper have been particularly influential in the developing of my understanding of tourism issues throughout my career. My friend Professor Bill Faulkner who, sadly, died while this book was at an early stage, contributed a great deal to my interest in complex tourism systems.

Noel Scott insisted that I think more deeply about some of the arguments in this book, and ensured that the figures which I had drafted are consistent and make some sort of sense.

Professor Dan Fasenmaier deserves particular mention for encouraging me to undertake this book, during a very pleasant stroll together in the Tyrol some years ago.

To all these, and my travelling companion over the years, I extend my thanks.

Eric Laws
London, 2004

Introduction

The central theme of *Improving Tourism and Hospitality Services* is rooted in the author's belief that the main issue for tourism and hospitality managers as the twenty-first century begins should be improving the nature and quality of experiences for the industry's clients, its staff and others affected by its operations.

Although these three groups of people have stakes in the creation and enjoyment of tourism and hospitality services, this book is mainly concerned with customer satisfaction. It is essential to provide customers with satisfying experiences from investments made in aircraft and hotels, airports and resorts, leisure facilities, shopping centres and tourist attractions, and for whom entrepreneurs have developed excursions, entertainment, activities and inclusive tours.

This book draws together several approaches to the study of tourist satisfaction, equating this with quality in tourism or hospitality services. It presents a series of case studies of situations which have caused problems resulting in customer dissatisfaction, where the quality of service provided has fallen short of expectations, for various reasons. Other case studies show how some of the industry's most successful organizations succeed in providing profitable services which their customers enjoy and return to as loyal customers knowing what standards of service to expect.

The cases were selected because they represent a turning point of some kind for each organization, or because they illustrate an innovative and effective approach to particular situations. But in each of the cases, decisions had to be taken by individual managers or teams, based on their own experience and insights, and in the light of the specific and unique circumstances confronting managers at that point in time.

Tourism services are complex, and often depend on the efforts of a network of specialist companies; their contributions to customer experiences can best be understood from a systems perspective. This approach highlights the appropriateness of the services they provide to tourists, the overall effects on workers and residents, and the interdependent nature of tourism enterprises. The tourism industry is a complex system because the organizations which contribute to it are extremely varied in several important characteristics. Some may be publicly owned while others are private companies. Many operate for a profit while others do not even charge for their services. Some provide the services they create directly to tourists, others act as wholesalers or agents for tourism principals. Some specialist companies are wholly dependent on tourism, others exist primarily to serve other client groups, but also cater to the specialized needs of tourists in the course of their main business activities. The scale of organizations operating in the tourism sector ranges from very small, proprietor-operated seasonal businesses such as guest houses, to international regulatory bodies such as IATA (the International Air Transport Association).

The analysis presented in this book summarizes and synthesizes a considerable body of research and technical literature dealing with operational aspects of tourism and hospitality, and several strands of contemporary management theory. The main areas include marketing, service industry theory, the literature on quality management, consumer choice, and some aspects of organizational behaviour and role theory. The theory reviewed in the book provides readers with a multidisciplinary base from which to understand the challenges and issues with which tourism and hospitality managers have to deal on an immediate basis as situations arise and change. The purpose of the theoretical discussion in this book is to establish a framework to evaluate the complex dynamics of customer satisfaction in tourism and hospitality.

This book is the outcome of nearly twenty years of my research into tourism management practices, problems and issues. It draws together some of my previous work, presented here in a more advanced and updated form intended for experienced managers and advanced students of hospitality and tourism management.

Improving Tourism and Hospitality Services is intended to help managers working in the hospitality and tourism industry, and to inspire students on advanced courses, who aspire to careers in tourism or hospitality, to contribute to the continuing improvement of services for all, with a stake in the success of this growing industry, whether they are staff, residents or tourists and guests. The quality of tourism services seems likely to become an ever more central factor for future managerial decisions. My purpose in writing this book is to provide a clear way of analysing services processes and experiences which will enhance readers' understanding of the service aspects of tourism and hospitality management.

Chapter 1 sets the contexts for studying tourism and hospitality service standards and introduces readers to the counter-intuitive approach taken here of analysing service failures (as well as examples of good practice) in order to understand the complex and dynamic nature of the industry.

Chapter 2 examines in some detail the interlinked factors contributing to satisfaction with tourism and hospitality services. The chapter also reviews the emergence and development of a distinct body of theoretical literature for service management, introducing the idea of service encounters between clients and staff as being centrally important in service quality outcomes. Systems theory and case study research are described and presented as suitable frameworks for the study of service management in tourism and hospitality.

Chapter 3 explains how service experiences can best be described and analysed. The consumerist gap approach is developed to show that consumers experience services as a series of events, comprising both technical features and service encounters. It is shown that any of these factors have the potential to depress the satisfaction a client experiences below the level he or she had expected when purchasing the service.

Chapter 4 is concerned with the ways in which a company provides services to its clients. The analysis of service delivery systems considers a variety of design and technical aspects as a prelude to the main focus of this chapter on the techniques of service blueprinting and service mapping. These are ways to identify the relationships between the technical design of a service, its staffing and customer outcomes. The chapter shows how they can be used diagnostically, to assist managers seeking ways to improve a functioning service, or as a research tool to test the validity of selected theories.

Chapter 5 reviews the literature on service quality and relates the concept to notions of customer satisfaction. This chapter includes a discussion of SERVQUAL and evaluates its important contributions to the development of services theory.

Chapter 6 takes a more traditional managerial stance and considers the significance of the marketing function in hospitality and tourism, particularly as it relates to customer expectations of service standards and consumer buying decisions.

Chapter 7 is entitled 'Improving tourism and hospitality service systems'. It places the discussion so far in the context of effective management of services and the difficulties to be recognized and overcome. The chapter includes some critical comments on certain contemporary approaches to the management of services such as those based on ISO 9000 documentation of processes, or on the minimization of staff–client interaction. It is recognized that the complex nature of the industry results in occasional problems, and the chapter provides an analysis of problem management and shows how crisis situations may be averted by skilled management and staff responses to difficulties experienced by clients.

Chapter 8 concludes the book with a more far-reaching discussion of organizational management issues for tourism and hospitality. It argues that too many theorists and managers approach their roles from outmoded and limited understanding of the dynamic and complex nature of challenges in the sector. The approach recommended in *Improving Tourism and Hospitality Services* is to place customers at the centre of organizational thinking rather than adopting a hierarchical and rigid view of the company's structure and its operations. The interdependent nature of the industry is discussed, and the chapter argues that it is beneficial to focus on networks and collaboration even within a very competitive marketplace if customer satisfaction is to be assured.

The book includes an appendix in the form of a set of slides for a management development workshop summarizing the main points in this book. An extensive and up-to-date bibliography is provided as a resource for those readers interested in conducting their own research into quality management issues and customer satisfaction in hospitality and tourism services.

CHAPTER 1

Service quality in tourism and hospitality

Introduction

This book deals with the challenges of managing tourism and hospitality businesses successfully so that they provide satisfying experiences for tourists and guests while profiting their owners. Rapert and Wren (1998: 223) claim that 'Service quality . . . (is now) an irrepressible, globally pervasive strategic force . . . as well as a key strategic issue on management's agenda.' World Tourism Organization (WTO) statistics indicate that 698 million people travelled abroad in 2000, many of them for leisure motivations, and some 10% of all jobs in the world are now related to tourism. Leisure travel is an integral component of the life-styles of large numbers of people in the developed world, and their activities affect many more who work or live in destination areas around the world. The prediction is that tourism, and the number of jobs supported by the industry, will continue to grow. The WTO predicts that in the year 2020 there will be 1.6 billion international tourist arrivals, based on projected annual growth rates of 4.3% each year. The highest levels of growth are expected to be in Asia, particularly in China, which is predicted to be the world's most popular destination in the year 2020 (WTO, 2002). China was ranked fifth most visited destination in 2000. During the first couple of years of the new millennium, several serious terrorist incidents have disrupted tourist activity around the world, but in the past the tourism industry has proved resilient to such problems, recovering fairly quickly both in destinations where incidents occurred, and as a global industry.

The overall economic significance of tourism is justification enough for attempts to analyse and improve its management techniques, but other reasons more relevant to the theme of this book relate to the highly competitive market conditions in which tourism businesses and destination authorities operate. Leisure travel is discretionary on the part of individual tourists: there are many alternative airlines, destinations, car rental companies, hotels, souvenir shops and activities, so it is essential to the success of individual enterprises that they understand how to provide their clients with the sorts of experiences which they want, as few customers will return to an unsatisfactory hotel, restaurant or destination. A similar but larger caution applies to the industry overall: the options for spending leisure time and discretionary money are not limited to tourism. Many people still prefer to take their holidays at home, perhaps renovating or redecorating their major financial asset, while acts of terrorism or merely the stresses of travel – recurrent delays and overcrowded conditions at airports, uncomfortable hotel rooms, illness from unaccustomed food or water and downright poor service experiences – have led some holidaymakers to decide not to travel again, at least for a while. However, it should be noted that the vast majority of the world's population have never travelled far from home, although this situation is rapidly changing, particularly in Asia.

Service standards have been problematic to travellers throughout history. Aristophanes' hero Dionysus consulted Heracles when planning his own journey to the underworld, requesting 'a list of the landladies with the fewest bedbugs', and the Roman satirist Martial complained that good drinking water was so scarce in the marshy area near Ravenna that it cost more than wine, as Casson (1994) notes in his study of travel in the ancient world. The standards of service continued to be a problem for travellers in the Middle Ages. Maczak (1995: 102) relates how one 'was once greatly amused in a German village when the servants brought him, in exchange for a tip, objects which passed for clean sheets, swearing that no one had recently slept in them except a ninety year old woman'.

The context to contemporary tourism service provision

In several important ways, tourism shares the general features of commercial and leisure life at the beginning of a new millennium, but it is important to realize at the outset that the interactions between tourists and their service suppliers which are analysed in this book are likely to continue to evolve. No detailed prediction of changes beyond the next few years can be made with any degree of confidence, yet the operating life for much of tourism's infrastructure and investment in resorts, hotels, airports, aircraft, and cruise liners spans several decades, or longer. Some preliminary comments follow which provide an overview of the contexts within which contemporary tourism markets operate.

The twentieth century, and particularly the second half of it, was a time of unprecedented change in many aspects of human life. The period includes a rapid shift from industrial employment, in the Western world at least, in favour of a range of service industries (Akehurst, 1996), supported by new capital-intensive technologies in transportation, communications and information processing, and a widespread improvement in the general standards of living, including longer paid holidays, better education and improved health (Ryan, 1991). These general factors combined with innovative business concepts, particularly the packaging of holidays, have made possible the rapid development of the mass market for leisure tourism. Linked to this, and another important driver of the development of the industry, are the sophisticated techniques used to target selected life-style and life-stage segments of the market (Ryan, 1995).

Another feature of the twentieth century was an increased aware-ness of consumer rights in societies which have become oriented towards market activities and where powerful business interests stim-ulate the consumption of an ever increasing variety of product types promoted as integral to culture and life-style preferences (McCracken, 1990; Prus, 1989). Consumer groups and government agencies have responded by demanding higher standards of reliabil-ity, safety, performance and social and environmental responsibility from manufacturers. This can be seen clearly in the various controls imposed progressively on the tobacco industry or in the shift by car manufacturers towards emphasizing safety and economy of opera-tion in the design and promotion of new models. A similar process is also evident in the services sector, but, as will be shown, the ways of regulating services and of managing their performance are not yet as clearly understood as is the case for tangible products. However, the academic and practitioner literature dealing with service quality management is growing rapidly in volume and increasing in the degree of sophistication shown in its analysis of these topics.

These trends are still evident; the beginning of the twenty-first century is therefore an interesting time to study the design and management of service quality. This book draws on the service management and quality management literature to provide an introduction to the main issues in understanding service quality, and it demonstrates how to analyse the processes which underlie tourism and hospitality services, with a particular focus on customers' experiences of them. Short case studies are provided to illustrate the issues and methods throughout the text.

Tourism and hospitality service failures

Although the objective of this book is to help the reader to understand service quality, the route taken is often counter-intuitive: the analysis of service failures casts light on both weaknesses and strengths in the systems under investigation. Failure is often both more apparent and more transparent than success! Analysis of the causes of failure casts light on the complex and dynamic nature of tourism services. One of the service researchers whose work has most influenced this book, Lynn Shostack, developed the blue-printing method of studying service design and delivery in response to the frustration she experienced in her role as a banking executive. She was particularly concerned to pull together all the elements of the service which had to operate simultaneously and consistently.

> Examples of poor service are widespread, in survey after survey services top the list in terms of consumer dissatisfaction . . . Faced with service problems, we tend to become somewhat paranoid. Customers are convinced that someone is treating them badly, managers think that recalcitrant individual employees are the source of the malfunction . . . No R and D departments laboratories or service engineers define and oversee the design. There is no way to ensure quality or uniformity in the absence of a detailed design. What piecemeal quality controls exist address only parts of the service. (Shostack, 1984: 133)

The quite high probability that something might go wrong with one of the many elements of a holiday, a journey or a stay in a hotel also leads to the need for managers to develop recovery programmes which go beyond correcting the immediate problem, by attending to customers' concerns (Mack *et al.*, 2000; Stauss, 2002).

In tourism, most sectors of the industry have regularly experienced a high incidence of complaints, including low standards during the journey between home and destination, poor accommodation, poor resort location and associated difficulties. A report discussed in Laws (1997) surveyed 11,500 British members of the Consumers' Association, asking them to rate the tour operators and countries they had patronized in the year to September 1996. The key criterion was 'whether they would definitely recommend them to a friend who wants to take the same sort of holiday'. Swiss Travel Service was the only operator of the 51 in the survey to gain a 'definitely' or 'probably' recommendation from all Consumers' Association respondents who had used the company. Poor accommodation was the main source of dissatisfaction; other concerns related to representatives, brochure accuracy, and changes to the arrangements once booked. Among the major tour operators' clients, the proportion surveyed who would 'definitely recommend' a particular tour operator ranged from only 48% for Thomson to a low of 25% for Airtours.

The Chief Executive of British Airways expressed the challenge in the following terms:

> Why not merely run an airline which is so good that it never has any problems? May I assure you that we are in a service business, and service businesses deal with people. There is never one perfect set of answers for dealing with people problems, otherwise they would not be people. What makes service businesses so interesting and so complex is that their prime stake in trade is people relations, and we are expected to handle those relations in the hurly burly of commerce, not in the quiet professionalism of a therapist's room. (Marshall, 1986: 10)

Sternlicht (2002) described 'The Sheraton Promise', a compensation programme for guests at any Sheraton hotel in the US or Canada who complain about one or more problems (see Table 1.1). A variety of levels of compensation are to be provided, following an apology. Staff participate in a role-play training session where they practise making an apology and offering compensation.

Table 1.1 *The main complaints from hotel guests*

- wrong type of room
- room not cleaned properly
- uncomfortable bed
- no wake up call
- slow service
- noise outside the hotel
- errors in the bill
- slow check-in
- reserved room not ready

Based on Sternlicht (2002)

Case studies

Case studies are common in tourism research (Prideaux, 2000), and are used in this book both to illustrate the nature of tourism service problems and successes, and also to demonstrate some of the methods available for researchers to use. The examples discussed here are drawn from various sectors of the tourism and hospitality industry, but often with a focus on airline service, the subject of my first research article (Laws, 1986). I continue to study airline service issues because of their intrinsic interest given the connotations of luxury and refinement generated by the prospect of airtravel, the difficulties of meeting passengers' service expectations within the special and confined conditions of a flight, and in the contexts of increasingly severe competition and the growing low cost flight sectors, and because much of the tourism industry is dependent on airtransportation. The case studies present and analyse specific situations at a particular time, but similar conditions could occur in any organization, and the examples described are not intended to be critical of any particular companies.

The first case study illustrates some of the issues which are analysed in this book.

CASE STUDY 1.1

The Edinburgh Airport buses

Some years ago I was working in Edinburgh, but commuted to my home in London most weekends. I became very familiar with the journey: one of the most irritating features was the Edinburgh airport bus service.

Turnhouse, Edinburgh's airport, is some miles from the city centre. As a result of the deregulation of public transport in Britain, two bus services linked the city centre and the airport's single terminal for scheduled passengers during the mid-1990s, a fleet of taxis is also based at the airport.

The airport bus services both start (or terminate) outside Waverley, Edinburgh's main railway station, proceed along Princes Street, and follow nearly identical routes through the suburbs and into the airport, where their stops are adjacent to one of the airport's two main check-in and arrival halls. The airport is quite small so passengers have only a couple of minutes' walk. Although there is no shelter outside the terminal, one or other of the services usually has a bus waiting and passengers seldom have to wait in the open.

Despite the apparent benefits of the airport bus system outlined above, at that time there were a number of weaknesses in the design concept for the service from the perspective of its customers.

- Any passengers joining the bus from Waverley station have to walk up a steep and rather narrow roadway used by taxis, then cross a busy road to reach the bus stops for the two services. As with the airport itself, one of the two buses is usually waiting.
- Both services have a number of request stops along their routes to the airport. However, although they follow similar routes, their stops are located at different points along the way. While it might seem beneficial in that more points are provided at which the airport bus services can be boarded, in fact, this presents passengers with three problems.
1 The drivers of both services tend to encourage passengers to buy a return ticket, citing its cost advantage over two singles.

However, neither service accepts the tickets of the other operator.

2 The bus stops in central Edinburgh all serve a variety of routes and operators. They carry quite small flags for each, often up to a dozen. The places where the airport services stop along the route are indicated by the bus numbers, and a small aircraft symbol, both of which can only be distinguished from close proximity; nor do they stand out from the other services. As a result it was not unusual to see people with heavy luggage pushing into shops to ask staff where they should wait for the bus.

3 The customer has to hail the airport buses at all intermediate stops. This is normal practice for British bus passengers, who are familiar with the requirement to watch for the approach of the service they require, and hail it by raising an arm prominently enough to attract the driver's attention. However, on a number of occasions when I have been a passenger customers have failed to stop an approaching airport bus. This seems to occur for three reasons.

i They are unaware that the airport bus does not automatically stop at indicated places along the route, and therefore do not hail the driver, who legitimately proceeds on his route. In one instance, an observant and sympathetic driver watching his rear view mirrors noticed his potential customers' consternation that the service had passed. He stopped his bus some 50 metres further along the road and waited for them. However, he proceeded to lecture his passengers on correct procedure, to their annoyance.

ii Congestion in Edinburgh's city centre often results in several buses driving close behind each other. When this happens clients are unable to see the destination boards of approaching buses, and consequently they fail to hail the service which they want. A variant on this problem is that the airport service drivers try to keep to their schedules, and in heavy traffic they tend to pull out from the lane used by general city buses queuing at the bus stops. The result is that waiting clients fail to spot the bus.

iii The third problem arises when a client waits at a bus stop indicating that airport buses can be boarded there, but hails a bus from the other company which uses an alternative stop. Even when the client establishes eye contact with the driver, the bus will not stop in these circumstances.

Discussion

This simple, descriptive case study demonstrates that the poor design of a service can undermine its customers' experience, and it highlights the need for systematic ways to analyse these problems. It can be imagined that more than one traveller has arrived at the airport late, and in a state of frustration, anxiety or anger, and some may have missed their flight because of the weaknesses in the bus service system.

Analysing tourism service quality

The foregoing discussion points to the need to develop further a theoretical understanding of service quality issues as they relate to tourism and hospitality. The argument around which this book revolves is that tourism managers can do much to mitigate dissatisfaction with tourism services by systematic, customer-focused approaches to the design and delivery of their organization's services. The approach is grounded in the consumerist gap concept (Laws, 1986) and in the techniques of service blueprinting (Shostack, 1984), perceptual blueprinting (Senior and Akehurst, 1992) and service mapping (Shostack and Kingman-Brundage, 1991). Services are best viewed as dynamic, complex systems with technical and service features within which clients and staff interact (Checkland and Scholes, 1990). This book emphasizes the significant link between the design and management of a company's services and the enjoyment of them by clients as the service is delivered; and it highlights the role of consumer judgement in evaluating those services. Therefore, it is critical for managers to understand their customers' perceptions of services.

The distinguishing features of its service styles are the power base on which an organization's image and its brands are built: these are the equity it has acquired with its customers, and they are the foundation for continuing client relationships. Therefore, the particular way in which the organization presents its service must be consistent, but that style must also evolve over time to remain appealing to consumers in the face of its competitors. Therefore, a theme which occurs throughout this book is the dynamic nature of tourism and hospitality services.

Kaye Chon, Editor of the *Journal of Travel Tourism Marketing*, pointed out at the Inaugural Martin Opperman Memorial Lecture that it is insufficient for a tourism firm to be merely excellent. Even though a particular hotel increased its satisfaction rating from 92% to 93% the following year, it actually slipped to second place that year because one of its competitors had been able to improve further the ways in which it served clients. There are different origins to the challenge of constantly improving service standards, based in the fluidity of consumer expectations and the rate of technological and entrepreneurial innovation in all spheres of producer–consumer activity, and also driven by the increased readiness of consumers to complain about purchases which do not provide the benefits and satisfactions they had anticipated.

The twin needs for consistent quality and constantly improving quality present a number of challenges for service organization managers. The root of the consistency problem is that the production and delivery of services involves many contributing actors, including not only staff, but also the customer. The academic work contrasting services with manufacturing is useful in clarifying this problem: to produce a car the manufacturer requires a wide range of components usually bought in from subcontractors. The characteristics of each of these components is closely specified, and they can be inspected or sampled for conformance before the car is assembled, using well-understood and very reliable techniques. The completed car can easily be inspected before being shipped to a dealer, who carries out further fine tuning before handing it to the paying customer. The client drives the car away, and the transaction has been completed. Apart from routine servicing the client usually has no further contact with the retailer until considering the purchase of another car, and importantly has had no interaction at all with the factory workers who assembled it. In tourism services, as this book demonstrates, the nature of the transaction is different. Service involves the interactions of staff and client during an extended time period.

Academic interest in service quality in tourism, although quite recent, is gathering pace (Fisk, Brown and Bitner, 1993). Laws, Buhalis and Craig-Smith (1999) identified eight titles dealing with quality management aspects of tourism out of a total of 380 books on tourism and related fields published in the decade since 1989. Hudson and Shephard (1998: 61–2) have argued that 'service quality has been increasingly identified as a key factor in differentiating service products and building a competitive advantage in tourism'. Discussing PhD research in Britain Baum (1998: 467) notes an increase in 'research with a focus on service quality'. The number of books dealing with service quality issues, particularly in tourism and hospitality, is increasing rapidly, as can be seen in the bibliography to this book. The bibliography also documents a large number of research articles (only a sample of the total to date) and shows that several academic journals specializing in this field of study have been established recently. This book represents a summary of my own understanding of tourism service quality gained over several decades of enjoying, working in, teaching and studying the tourism industry.

Conclusion

This chapter has indicated that tourism is a major global industry, that it is very susceptible to customer confidence levels, and that it is a complex industry. Aside from the concerns about safety, the future of individual firms and destinations, and of the whole industry, depends on providing tourists and guests with satisfying experiences. One tourist's experience is created by numerous organizations, each offering a variety of activities and functions, but together contributing to an overall package (Laws, 1997; Kandampully, 2000). It is not surprising that our understanding of service quality issues in tourism, and therefore of how to improve tourism and hospitality services, is in a state of flux and undergoing rapid development (Cronin and Taylor, 1992; Ekinci and Riley, 1999; Hill and Alexander, 2000). Indeed, the rapid development of service theory is occurring right across the service sector (Gummesson, 1999; Brady and Robertson, 2001; Imrie, Cadogan and McNaughton, 2002).

The problem explored in this book is not a simple binary question, is this or is this not a 'good' service? It will become apparent that my view is that customers experience a range of satisfaction with any service. Rather the issues are about the extent to which the service is satisfying or not satisfying, and the analysis recognizes that both responses can occur during one service. This approach deals in fuzzy categories. These have been described in terms of vagueness (Sainsbury, 1990). Keefe and Smith (1999:16) argue that the best 'criterion of vagueness [focuses] directly on the lack of any sharp boundaries rather than on borderline cases'.

The cases described in this book are discussed in terms of existing theory and explore emerging service and quality management theory. The overall objective of this book is to assist readers in understanding how aspects of tourism and hospitality services affect client satisfaction, and to show what can be done either to avoid problems in service experiences, or to improve further their design and delivery.

CHAPTER 2

Tourism and hospitality service quality research

Introduction

A desire to understand service quality in tourism service systems underlies this book. A useful starting point is the contrast between the reliability of modern manufactured products where a failure can confidently be predicted not to occur before several million operating cycles, compared with service delivery systems where it is less certain that criteria for standards can be achieved consistently, or indeed that customers will be satisfied with the service.

The difficulty revolves around the fact that there are two roots to services, termed 'Type A' and 'Type B' (Laws, 1986). The technical aspects of managing equipment and materials (Type A management) require different skills from managing the interactions between staff and clients (Type B service management). It is important to note that both types of skill are needed to deliver quality services (Siha, 1999). Differing though connected implications flow from a recognition of these two factors in service management and service consumption. While Type A factors are generally under the direct control of managers, the Type B factors are more complex, less predictable and less amenable to precise control. Type B factors include the role specifications, skills and motivations of staff, including their personal ability to interact effectively with clients, but a high degree of unpredictability results from the variable expectations and behaviour which different clients bring to the service episode and its constituent elements. Role theory is a somewhat underemployed approach in the tourism management literature, but as Katz and Kahn (1978) and Chenet, Tynan and Money (1999) have shown, it can provide deep insights into both consumer and staff behaviour.

Each type of service such as banking, restaurants, hotels or airlines has its own operational characteristics, different in specific ways from those of other sectors. Chase (1978) drew another important distinction between services in which customer contact is a frequent occurrence, and those where contact points are minimized. The minimization of contact points makes it simpler to specify and control the delivery of a service and offers benefits such as a reduction in staff costs. The weaknesses associated with this approach in the context of tourism management are a recurring theme throughout this book.

Allwein (1996) and Craig (2000) have discussed the insights offered by various types of diagram in business and research contexts. Figure 2.1 illustrates the relationships between the basic factors contributing to tourists' satisfaction. Whether or not a customer is satisfied with his or her journey can be conceptualized as a balance between the service the traveller anticipated and that experienced. It will be shown later that various factors lead to expectations of the service, notably the way it is advertised, any previous experience the customer may have had with the company or its competitors, and comments from friends and family regarding their experiences. 'Word of mouth' recommendations or criticisms can be influential in determining the customer's attitudes prior to the service.

Noe (1999) provides an insightful review of the concept of tourist satisfaction and its development in contemporary tourism research literature. In summary, satisfaction is assessed by stepping away from the experience, and evaluating it. A number of factors such as the consumer's emotional state, psychographics and social environment influence the judgement, which is essentially a comparison of expectations with experience rather than a measurement of absolute service performance. The judgement is about the extent to which expectations have been met, and therefore satisfaction is dependent on what the customer knows about the service and the service provider as well as the actual delivery of the service.

Two main sets of factors determine the customer's actual experiences. These are firstly the technical resources used to create the service, and secondly the way that the service is delivered to the customer, notably the interactions with staff which occur during the various events of the service process.

From this perspective, service quality is a key link between the organization and the outcomes of its activities, particularly its profitability (Heskett et al., 1994; Zeithmal, 2000), customer loyalty (Berger and Nasr, 1998; Bloemer, de Ruyter and Wetzels, 1999),

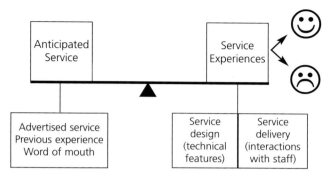

Figure 2.1 *The factors contributing to tourists' satisfaction*

employee satisfaction (Ross, 1993; Loveman, 1998; Gutek *et al.*, 2000), and productivity (Schmenner, 1995; Chenet, Tynan and Money, 1999; van der Wiele, Boselie and Hesselink, 2002). Grönroos (1990) argues that service quality comprises two fundamental components – technical quality ('what' is delivered) and functional quality ('how' the service is delivered) – with an important third component, the organization's image. If the quality of tourism or hospitality services could be determined solely and completely by managerial decisions, then all clients participating in one service episode should experience it in similar ways. The fact that this often does not happen can be illustrated from analysis of customers' correspondence to their service provider following some problem, or generated by research through focus group methods and from our individual experiences. Assuming that all passengers in a particular class on one flight were in fact offered identical service, any remaining differences they report in the satisfaction which they experienced could be ascribed to any or all of three major variables. These are their individual attitude at the time, their involvement (enthusiasm) for travel by air, and differences in their prior experience of similar services (Estelami, 2000; Bateson, 2002; Sparks, 2002). Some financial analysts, in the face of this complexity and the apparent cost of responding to or compensating dissatisfied customers, argue that customer satisfaction should not be a matter of concern to investors or senior managers (Williams and Visser, 2002). I totally reject the validity of this instrumental, one-sided, short-term view.

The distinguishing characteristics of tourism services

Before considering these issues in more detail, it will be helpful to examine the special nature of service sector transactions. It has been suggested that the early objective of service research (prior to about 1980) was to establish the significant distinctions between the sector and the manufacturing of products (Fisk, Brown and Bitner, 1993). Many researchers, such as Cowell (1986), have studied these problems, summarized in Table 2.1.

A variety of tests have been proposed for tangibility, ranging from whether the purchase can be touched (services cannot) and the degree of difficulty which clients experience in understanding the nature of

Table 2.1 *Differences between manufacturing and services*

Manufacturing characteristic	Meaning	Service characteristic	Service feature
Tangibility	Customer can test-drive a car	Intangibility	The customer cannot sample a service before purchasing it
Separability	Customer is not involved in manufacturing the car	Inseparability	The customer is part of the service and interacts directly with the organization and its staff during the service
Homogeneity	Each car is identical to others produced to a given specification	Heterogeneity	A particular service may be experienced differently by each client
Storability	Most new cars are stored for weeks or months prior to sale and delivery	Perishability	The organization cannot put an unsold service into storage

their purchase (Bateson, 1977; Berno and Bricken, 2001). In reality most purchases have both tangible and intangible aspects, and so are located somewhere between the two extremes of this consumption–tangibility continuum. The significance for this book of characterizing tourism and hospitality as largely intangible lies in the consequent difficulty for clients of judging the outcomes of a service transaction and consequent problems for service managers.

The service characteristic which is most salient to this book is *inseparability*. The essential feature of services is the interaction required between the customer and client-contact staff to create and to deliver a service (Rathmell, 1966; Czepiel, Solomon and Surprenant, 1985; Bateson, 2002). Grönroos (1982) has argued that inseparability causes marketing and production to be highly interactive. It is widely recognized that services are performed with the participation of the customer, and the inseparability of production and consumption means that each service interaction is in some respects unique. For example, the American company Federal Express defined its service as 'all actions and reactions that customers perceive they have purchased' (Lovelock, 1994). The interaction between customer and service provider has been identified as perhaps the major constraint on the efficiency of a service delivery system (Chase, 1978; Grönroos, 1998).

Cowell (1986:25) wrote of heterogeneity: 'even though standard systems may be used, for example to handle a flight reservation . . . each unit of service may differ from other units.' Everyone experiences a given service differently due to their differing personalities, any previous experience of the type of service, its importance or urgency to them on the present occasion, their moods and so on. The general notion of heterogeneity was illustrated by the two faces in Figure 2.1. One customer is pleased with the service, while another is disappointed with his or her experience of the same service.

CASE STUDY 2.1

The variability of tourists' service experiences

A group of students travelling from a UK university to the Mediterranean for a study visit participated in a questionnaire survey to determine the range of satisfaction they experienced during the scheduled flights. Two short self-completion question-naires were designed to solicit their views (based on constructs which had been identified as relevant to passenger satisfaction during earlier research). Basic biographical details were sought, including their prior experience of flights, and respondents were then asked to rank some 20 aspects of the flight on a seven-point Likert scale. The final item asked them to rate the flight overall. The scales ranged from Extremely Dissatisfying to Extremely Satisfying. The neutral case was phrased for respondents to indicate that their experience of that aspect of the journey matched what they had anticipated.

A total of 31 usable replies were received from the 42 travellers. The criteria for a usable reply was strict: both outbound and return questionnaires had to be returned by any individual, with all questions completed. On the outbound flight, 29 of the 31 indicated that overall the flight had met their expectations. Four considered the return flight marginally better than the outbound, two thought it rather better, but two stated that they found it rather less satisfying. The other 23 considered it about as satisfying as the outbound flight.

Discussion
This simple finding illustrates the complexity of matching all passengers' expectations within the physical and technical constraints of a flight. The study confirms that people receiving one service will experience it differently, and therefore the quality of that service cannot be construed as managerially determined.

Perishability is a significant managerial problem in tourism. Its meaning is that a service such as an unsold hotel room for a particular night or an airline seat on a specific departure cannot be stockpiled for sale at a later date. Most service sectors, including hotels, restaurants and tourist attractions, experience the problem of perishability and also have to deal with the converse difficulties resulting from peak period demand and congestion. The typical response is to discount prices as departure dates approach, or to charge a premium for peak season travel. These policies have been very successful in stimulating sales and smoothing peak demand, but there are also some detrimental consequences which are discussed later.

Some authors have proposed a fifth factor distinguishing services from manufactures – *ownership* – but it has limited relevance to the issues examined here. Its meaning is that the customer does not obtain a legal title to objects as a result of purchasing access to service facilities. Cowell (1986) points out that people attending a theatre do not purchase their seat in the sense that they could take it away with them after the performance. Similarly, hotel guests have access to their room only during the period they have paid for, and have no legal right to take towels or other room furnishings home with them!

It is not unusual to find a notice in hotel rooms to this effect, sometimes listing the price of desirable items such as a bathrobe, and pointing out that a new one could be purchased from the hotel. On the other hand, a small memento of their stay may be important to some guests, for example when on their honeymoon, and most companies budget for some 'shrinkage'. Early in my career, when I went to interview the managing director of a well-known tour operator, he pointed out the display in his private office of over a hundred good quality glass and ceramic ashtrays bearing the names and logos of some of the most renowned hotels in the world!

The challenge of managing services

The distinctions noted above were important in helping the development of a separate field of study for services, and helped identify several general challenges facing service managers, summarized in Table 2.2. These are discussed further at relevant points throughout this book.

In summary, it had become clear by the 1980s that services were more complex, more variable and less easy to control than manufacturing due to two key differences:

1. The ability to reduce (or even eliminate) production staff judgements in manufacturing production processes.
2. The absence of direct customer involvement in manufacturing production.

Table 2.2 *Contrasted management challenges in manufacturing and services*

	Manufacturing	Services
Consistent performance	Variances between models are minimized during manufacturing	Customer interaction with staff during service delivery makes it hard to achieve precise standards
Conformance to specification	Can be achieved through monitoring and sampling	Responsiveness to individual preferences are a feature of many services
Variegated product lines	Easy for manufacturers to segment their markets by offering different performance characteristics and specifications	Different levels of service are offered to each class of client at one time
Communicating performance features	Easy for manufacturers to specify performance or luxury features	Imagery- and lifestyle-based marketing appeals do not distinguish service features

Myopia in managing services

Despite these academic findings, there is evidence suggesting that some contemporary service managers continue to attempt to apply either or both of these manufacturing-based methods, and this has resulted in a number of mistaken approaches to the management of tourism services (Grönroos, 1998; Laszlo, 1999). One example is the trend to automate some aspects of hotel operations. Automated transactions are a way of reducing staff involvement, and are familiar to bank customers in the form of cash dispensing machines. These give the great convenience of 24-hour banking, and have become widely accepted since their introduction in the 1970s. In tourism, some hotels which do not provide a night service now issue guests with a code for the keyless outer door lock by which they gain access to the building at night, but delegates at a tourism conference in Munich in 1999 told their colleagues with some anger about the entry lock which had failed to accept their code when they returned after a late night function. They had phoned the proprietor but he had refused to get out of bed to assist them, until they called the police!

Automation is becoming more prevalent in tourism: most travellers are familiar with machines which issue travel tickets at railway stations or for urban transit systems. Automation is not the fundamental weakness of the situation described above. The problem is that the system does not fully recognize the variability of human behaviour, or our emotional responses to situations. The manager's refusal to assist his (paying) guests turned a simple technical problem into a service disaster. Technology can assist some of the routine procedures travellers have to deal with by simplifying and speeding up some elements of the service process. It is increasingly common to bypass airport check-in lines by swiping a frequent traveller or credit card through a machine which issues a boarding pass (often including a seat number) for passengers with a confirmed booking. At some airports, passengers arriving on international flights can also bypass the normal immigration check if they hold a machine-readable identity card, although they are still subject to a possible customs inspection.

In contrast to these attempts to simplify and speed up airport procedures to the benefit of both passengers and the airlines and airport authorities, security procedures have become more rigorous in response to recent terrorist incidents. This has the unfortunate effect of increasing the amount of time a traveller has to spend in the airport, and causing long queues and delays, especially at peak travel times. Prior to the terrorist attacks on the USA on 11 September 2001, it was quite possible to check in for most international scheduled flights less than an hour prior to departure. A year later, many airlines and airports require passengers to check in two hours or more beforehand in case of delays due to the increase in security measures. Exacerbating the consequent frustration of travellers, many airport operators, not least BAA (British Airports Authority), are increasing the proportion of floor space devoted to retail facilities resulting in even more congested and uncomfortable conditions airside.

Service encounters – moments of truth

Much of what customers notice and judge during a service is the contact they have with the service staff who deliver the technical features of the service. Czepiel, Solomon and Surprenant (1985), in an important edited collection of research which has not received as much attention as it merits, call this the 'service encounter'. Normann (1991) referred to the points of interaction in a service episode as 'moments of truth', a phrase which Carlzon (1987) had adopted from the consultant for the title of his perceptive book reflecting on his experiences managing the Scandinavian tour operator Vingressor and its parent airline, SAS. Both Carlzon and Normann have demonstrated that each of the moments of truth is an occurrence used by customers to judge the overall quality of the service and the organization. In complex services, such as undertaking a journey or going on a holiday, it is not just the main organization's staff who provide services to clients; subcontracting organizations also have direct contact with the client, raising further issues for managers dealing with partners in the service chain. In the case of a tour operator, clients are actually served by transport companies, hotels, restaurants and a variety of tourist attractions in the destination. As each of these organizations may also supply services to other (competing) tour operators it is not surprising that a client experiences varying styles and qualities of service during his or her holiday.

The concept of 'moments of truth' and the issues surrounding service experiences and service encounters between clients and staff are discussed throughout this book.

Theoretical frameworks for tourism and hospitality service research

Systems theory perspective

A systems approach is fundamental to both the consumerist gap concept and to service blueprinting. Three stages can be identified in general models of system processes. Firstly, inputs are required in the form of equipment, skills, resources and clients' demands for the industry's outputs, holiday packages or hotel stays. But, a system's outputs also include the profit and work which it creates, and the effects of its operations on other interests, notably those of the destination's residents. The intermediate stage of systems analysis connecting inputs with outputs, is concerned with the internal processes whereby organizations transform those inputs into outputs. Kast and Rosenzweig (1985) have shown that an organization consists of smaller subsystems (departments) acting within the larger environment. The various components or elements of the system are interlinked, and the efficiency of the system operating within its boundary will be affected by changes to any of the elements of which it is composed. In general, a system can be described as an ordered set of components; each component is affected by being part of the system: its behaviour is constrained by the needs and conditions of its setting, and the entire system is affected if one component changes. Taking a view of a system is to recognize that particular system's boundaries; setting a clear boundary around the system under investigation emphasizes the inputs and outputs for investigation. Outside the boundary of any system are a range of other entities which influence its activities, and which are affected by them: the system is itself part of the environment for other systems. Proponents of systems analysis also recognize the need for an organization to monitor the external environment within which it operates. The network of supplier and support organizations with which tourist organizations typically interact is examined in subsequent chapters.

For effective management of a tourism system to take place, two aspects need to be clearly understood: the effects on outputs of any change to its inputs, and secondly the ways in which its processes are organized and controlled. Control over the quality and consistency of a system's outputs requires regular monitoring of its products, and an effective feedback channel between the monitoring and decision-making subsystems within the organization.

Business organizations can be seen as purposeful social systems, taking resources from their environment and using the skills of their employees to produce outputs to satisfy their clients and the organization's own objectives. Although the systems approach can be applied to the separate operating units of the industry, such as tour operators, travel retailers, airlines, hotels, and tourist attractions at destinations, it is at its most powerful when focused on the complex issues of destinations (Laws, 1995) or, as in this book, the entire industry. A systems approach enables the goals, organization, resource and output decisions of management to be examined, in order to understand the effects of their decisions on other groups affected by the organization's activities. Constraints such as competition and regulatory environments may also be studied to understand how levels of efficiency are effected in the industry. Figure 2.2 shows how these systems concepts can be applied to the inclusive holiday industry.

The holiday industry system

The holiday industry system consists of destination elements (or sub-systems) in the form of natural or primary destination attractions, such as the area's climate, its scenery or an important castle, supported by secondary features such as hotels, guest houses and the range of attractions, shopping and catering in the city centre. These interact with transport, tour operating and travel retailing subsystems to provide the entire range of services required for a holiday.

The model recognizes the significance of external factors such as changing competitive conditions, or improvements to the transport

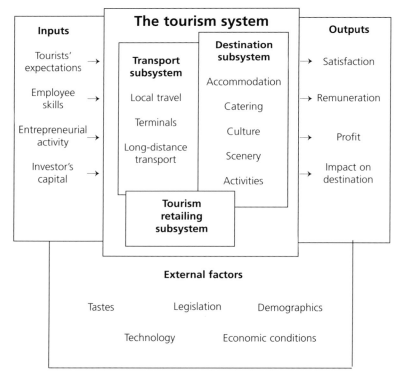

Figure 2.2 *The tourism industry system*

network. The method focuses attention on the outcomes of the system's functioning for particular stakeholder groups during a given time period. Evaluation of the outcomes against the costs of inputs and policy objectives provides the basis of feedback, thus introducing a future-time dimension to the model.

Kaspar (1989) has recommended the systems approach in analysing tourism because it encourages the abandonment of one-dimensional thinking so that multiplex factors can be recognized and analysed from a variety of disciplinary perspectives. Interest is focused on psychological, economic, social, technological, political and ecological contexts to tourism management decisions. He pointed out that a theoretical image of reality can be gained in three ways: by reductionistic, holistic or systemic approaches. Reductionism dissects a whole entity into separate, isolated units (others have called this approach 'atomization'), but that method places the focus on the elements of a system, rather than the interrelationships between them. Holism represents the contrary approach; its proponents regard the whole as non-separable and therefore non-analysable. Neither of these are particularly helpful approaches. Kaspar (ibid.: 444) quoted Kuhne's view that these limitations are sufficient to abandon both approaches and to search for 'a perspective which enables one to grasp the peculiarities of the whole and the specific properties of the parts at the same time'.

The consumerist gap concept and the methodologies discussed later represent an attempt to follow Kuhne's precept, in bringing a systems-theoretic perspective to the study of service quality management in tourism. The systems approach is interested in the interactions of its components, and when people are a significant factor in the way clients experience the outputs of an organization, a systems approach is particularly appropriate. The argument that selected inputs are combined in a series of processes with the intention of producing specified outputs suggests that efficiency in the system's operation can be evaluated by measuring outputs against the inputs required to produce them, by examining the quality of those outputs, and by considering the way each process contributes to the overall service. Similarly, marketing planning and consumer behaviour models incorporate a feedback loop (or loops) – a mechanism by which consumers are able to express their opinions of a company's current market offering. Feedback provides a basis for the producer to modify future output: a closer match to consumer expectations may be obtained by assessing their opinions of a product's features or performance in the contexts of changing technology, and competitors' innovations. The issue touched on here – the evolution of tourism products and services – is considered at a later stage in this book.

The various components or elements of the system are interlinked, and the efficiency of the system operating within its boundary will be affected by changes to any of the subsystems of which it is composed or the processes they employ. The systems view of any organization emphasizes that it exists to carry out the activities and processes related to achieving its aims. Furthermore, it controls its activities and interacts with the environment in order to obtain resources and attract support for its products. In a competitive and constantly developing industry, effective service management means a relentless pursuit of new goals of quality improvement.

Two sets of ideas underlie systems thinking:

> emergence and hierarchy, and communication and control. Each identifiable (i.e. emergent) system thus has within it a series (or hierarchy) of subsystems that are in themselves complete . . . each level in the hierarchy has its own distinct emergent properties which are only appropriate at that level of analysis. (Kirk, 1995: 18)

The analysis of tourism services as a system also gives the advantage of identifying the main groups of people acting in it, or influenced by it: particularly the managers, staff and tourists. The systems view provides a framework to understand the effects of the system's operation on them and other stakeholders, such as the residents of a destination area (Berno and Bricken, 2001). If the system inputs are the expectations and spending of clients, the skills and attitudes of staff, and the resources and skills of management, then the appropriateness and effectiveness of the system design and its operation can be assessed by comparing the system inputs with the outcomes for each stakeholder group, that is the satisfaction experienced by clients of the system and the remuneration, work satisfaction and career development of staff. Profit and growth of the organization can be regarded as proprietors' and managerial outcomes. While these outcomes are accepted as important for staff and managers, this study is predominantly concerned with outcomes for clients, and it is the significance of those for organizational success which provides the feedback loop making the argument iterative.

Hard and soft systems theory

Checkland and Scholes (1990), Patching (1990), Kirk (1995) and Ingram (2000) are among those who have noted that although systems thinking has mainly been applied to 'hard' engineering situations, where outcomes are unambiguous and highly predictable, the concept can also be applied in 'soft' situations, where human behaviour is a significant factor in business activities combining social and technical processes.

It is central to the argument in this book that services have both technical features (Type A), and service components (Type B) in which passengers interact with the staff who deliver the service. The Type A analysis is comparable to 'hard systems' which specify the technology of a productive system to meet clear performance objectives. In contrast, 'soft systems' recognize the Type B, people-related problems which are less structured, and where the outcomes of actions are less predictable. These are termed 'messy' problems (Checkland and Scholes, 1990).

> Problem situations, for managers, often consist of no more than a feeling of unease, a feeling that something should be looked at, both from the point of view of whether it is the thing to do and in terms of how to do it. [The soft systems method] is a system of enquiry. In it, a number of notional systems of purposeful activity which might be relevant to the problem situation are defined, modelled and compared with the perceived problem situation in order to articulate a debate about change, a debate which takes in both whats and hows. (Ibid.: 1)

The early studies by these authors confronted the difficulty that in ill-defined problem situations it was not possible to answer the questions, 'what is the system?', and 'what are its objectives?' Explaining the way in which progress was made, Checkland and Scholes identified one feature which all had in common, 'They all featured human beings in social roles, trying to take purposeful action.'

Qualitative research and case studies

The foregoing discussion has noted that tourism services are complex and that analysis has to deal with peoples' feelings and behaviour during service processes. This raises the question of how to analyse tourism services. Gummesson (1991: 180) has observed that 'theories concerned with processes in organizations must primarily be generated on the basis of real data, and not by logical deduction from established theory'. Other researchers have discussed how tourism researchers face the need to 'utilize diverse forms of evidence and information when the feelings of people are being studied . . . in order to deal with such phenomena, scholars and practitioners often employ intuitive and subjective evidence which is emic, not etic, in nature' (Walle, 1997: 525 and 534).

When the research objective is the exploration of relationships and concepts, rather than verifying existing hypotheses, qualitative research methods including case research are recommended (Neuman, 1994; Parkhe, 1993; Bonoma, 1985). Eisenhardt (1989: 534) defines the case study method as 'a research strategy which focuses on understanding the dynamics present within single settings' where multiple sources of evidence could be used. In addition, Bonoma (1985: 203) emphasizes the significance that case study methods depend on multiple data sources for the real-life context in which management's acts occur. Yin (1994) argued that multiple case studies should be regarded as multiple experiments posing the issue of replicability, informed by preliminary concepts derived from earlier case work, whereas case studies of single situations are specific, and contextualized by their setting.

Case studies of service problems

Many of the case studies discussed in this book deal with problems experienced in tourism services. This interest in negative aspects of service management and service experiences requires explanation. The justification is in four parts. It is often difficult for clients to explain why a particular service was pleasing, but most people seem able to express their views clearly and vigorously when things go wrong. Table 2.3 shows the number of passengers who wrote voluntarily to an airline either complaining or praising the flight they had taken.

Table 2.3 *Complaints and compliments to an airline during one month*

Letters received	3,623
Of which:	
Complaints	2,445
Compliments	696
Queries about the service	482

Source: Laws (1991)

A second justification is that the problematic features of service experiences provide material for discussion and analysis, and can also be a basis for enhancements to service design or service delivery in the future.

A third factor is that organizations need to market distinctive sets of benefits to offer their customers in order to have a clear position in the marketplace among competitors providing very similar basic or core functions. The strategies which they can adopt to achieve a powerful position include pricing, branding and service style.

A fourth consideration is that the related topics of service quality, customer satisfaction and the design and delivery of services are not static. As indicated in Figure 2.3, five types of pressure make this a dynamic field of study. The lightning shapes in the figure imply complex and indirect pressures acting on the existing 'service design 2003' resulting in the revised/improved 'service design 2005'. Changing technology, competitors' improvements to their services and customers' expressed preferences for different styles of service produce a climate in which managers expect to adapt their ways of doing business at regular intervals, and within which they exercise their creative flair to meet new market opportunities. Succeeding chapters will extend the discussion of service design, and review a number of strategies which companies can take to achieve the goal of providing customer satisfaction.

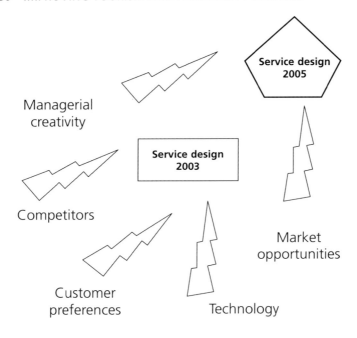

Figure 2.3 *Development pressures on service design*

Conclusion

There is a general consensus in the research community that tourism services are complex, and that any aspect can contribute to the success or failure of a service. Despite this, much current thinking is hindered by a mechanical and linear approach to services which probably stems from two root causes: inappropriate ways of thinking about services, and their complexity. Firstly, the 'first generation' approach to services noted by Normann (1991) persists; its attraction to many managers and researchers lies in its reference to experience transferred from the manufacturing sector where management decisions about design and manufacturing control result in logically predictable outcomes. Much of the current thinking about tourism service quality reflects themes in economic theory which exhibit a preference for mathematical analysis of a set of forces tending to stability and equilibrium, in contrast to the heterogeneous, dynamic forces tending to greater diversity and increasing complexity in tourism, which can probably be more realistically modelled through chaos theory (Faulkner and Russell, 1997; Gleick, 1987).

Secondly, transactions in tourism service systems do not have the directness of results which characterizes modern mass produced goods and the processes of their production. Equifinality is a key concept in systems theory; it recognizes that given inputs into complex processes may result in differing outcomes (Bertalanffy, 1968). The lack of relative certainty for tourism quality arises from human involvement in the service delivery processes, both as consumers and as producers, further compounded by the roles of individual expectations and perceptions in service judgements making consensual evaluation of service quality problematic.

CHAPTER 3

Analysing service experiences in tourism and hospitality

Introduction

Tourism is an industry which is concerned with transporting people on a temporary basis away from their homes to other places where they stay for a while and indulge in a range of pursuits before returning home. Holidays are generally expensive and people tend to be somewhat anxious about visiting new locations so they are often in a rather apprehensive frame of mind when they embark on a journey. The test for hospitality and tourism enterprises is whether they can provide their clients with experiences which are enjoyable and satisfying, but the nature of the industry is such that events sometimes make it difficult to please clients. The purpose of this chapter is to explore some of these issues and to provide an understanding of the factors which impinge upon tourism service experiences.

This chapter introduces the consumerist gap technique of researching service experiences, particularly to investigate problems in a service. The consumerist gap utilizes a number of methodologies to understand customers' experiences of services, including critical incident techniques, content analysis of customer comments and correspondence, and observation diaries. The consumerist gap concept highlights the significance of customer dissatisfaction to a company's survival. It was developed to analyse mismanaged passenger experiences following a technical failure in an airline service (Laws, 1986).

Events in tourists' experiences

Travellers often express overall satisfaction or dissatisfaction with an airline journey, but more detailed analysis shows that every service is actually experienced by the client as a series of events (Johnston,

1995; Yasin and Yavas, 1999; Tribe, 2002). This is illustrated in Figure 3.1: it might be imagined that the cascading boxes represent filing cards recording more detail of each event.

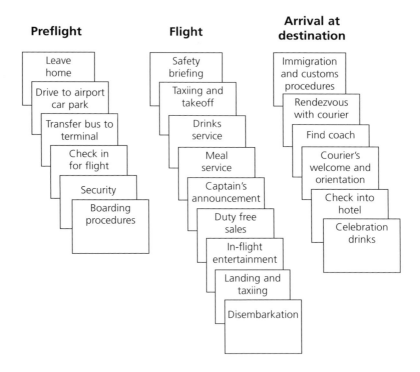

Figure 3.1 *Sequence of events in a journey*

The consumerist gap conceptualizes a service episode as consisting of a series of events. Each event has an outcome for the client in terms of varying satisfaction levels compared by that person to his or her anticipated satisfaction. Clients' experiences during each event of a service episode may therefore be measured along a continuum ranging from 'very satisfied' to 'very dissatisfied'. This continuum forms the vertical axis of the consumerist gap diagram shown in Figure 3.2.

In the consumerist gap model shown in Figure 3.2, A_0 represents the level of service which clients anticipated at the time of purchase

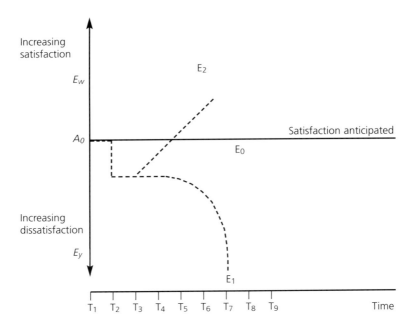

Figure 3.2 *The consumerist gap (based on Laws, 1986)*

(see Clow *et al.*, 1997 for a discussion). The satisfaction they experience during the delivery of a service is tracked by the paths E_1 and E_2. E (the satisfaction experienced) can be higher or lower than anticipated (A_0) as the various events in the service unfold. The assumption is that the company passes its acid test of consumer satisfaction when an individual's anticipated level of service as measured by E is indeed experienced, and $E = A_0$. By definition, this occurs at the outset of a service, and it is a measure of managerial success (the acid test) to return satisfaction to this level after any problems.

When service standards are higher than anticipated, consumers are very satisfied, and at level E_w positive outcomes include compliments to staff and favourable personal recommendations of the company to friends or colleagues by clients. The opposite extreme, when the service standards fail to meet the clients' expectations, is characterized by their increasing discomfort, frustration and ill-will. This situation can result from unscheduled interruptions to a journey, or from unsatisfactory performance of service events. Such problems are recorded at E_y where individual clients experience so much discomfort that they complain.

The horizontal axis of the model is calibrated in time units (T_1 ... T_n) during which the service episode evolves. Initially, satisfaction is at the level anticipated, and the service proceeds smoothly. But if an interruption or other failure occurs, satisfaction falls below the anticipated level and the company responds by seeking technical solutions to restore normal service. In the model this occurs at time T_2, when a gap in consumer satisfaction is opened. The depth of the gap below A_0 reflects the degree of dissatisfaction which the consumer has experienced.

The sequence and intensity of the company's responses to any technical (Type A) problems during a service affect clients' satisfaction and are a particular concern of this analysis. It takes some time to marshal the resources needed to overcome failure, and this takes the model to T_3, when the company begins to correct the problem. At the same time service responses (Type B) are needed to restore customers' confidence or overcome their anxieties and discomfort. If these responses are inappropriate, by T_4 their dissatisfaction will have deepened. However, with effective action the model shows that technical (Type A) problems have been overcome and the normal service is resumed by time T_5. The final level of satisfaction depends on how clients' needs were met by Type B responses during the interruption episode. Appropriate Type B responses can bridge the consumerist gap, even building greater customer satisfaction than had been anticipated. These are shown in path E_2. In contrast, path E_1 tracks the result of inappropriate actions which deepen the dissatisfaction experienced by clients.

The consumerist gap conceptual model charts the ensuing fluctuations in customers' satisfaction levels, and continues by postulating an 'acid test': whether a passenger would purchase another service from that company. Table 3.1 shows that flights which passed the acid test seem to share one of two main characteristics, either they were mainly satisfying, or they showed evidence that any dissatisfying experience had been well handled in the subsequent part encounter. In contrast, in flights which failed this acid test the passenger either experienced predominantly satisfaction depressants, or one unsatisfactory part encounter or event overrode any satisfaction boosters he or she experienced. To the extent that each of the clients felt that a company had failed their personal acid test, its future success could be jeopard-

Table 3.1 *Consumerist gap acid test of flights*

Pass	• Those on which passengers experienced no significant problems
	• Those where any problem was perceived to be handled well
Fail	• Problems which occurred were unresolved during the flight
	• Initial problems (usually technical) were exacerbated (usually by poor service encounters).

ized through direct loss of business and as a consequence of critical comments made to friends, relatives or colleagues.

The consumerist gap concept represents a concern to gain an understanding of the customers' perceptions of the factors which are significant in their evaluation of service quality, and it may be contrasted to other approaches which tend to focus on technical and managerial perspectives such as those expounded in a series of papers by Parasuraman, Zeithmal and Berry (notably in 1985, 1988 and 1990). Their influential service-gaps approach is discussed in a subsequent chapter of this book.

Satisfaction boosters and depressants

The outcome of each event may boost or depress customer satisfaction, but the intangible nature of services makes it hard for the client to judge what to expect, or to know how to assess what was received.

> In most service encounters, there are few or no natural clues to utility, either before the service occurs or after it is accomplished. Often, the customer does not know how to tell when she or he would be satisfied, and managers do not know how to structure the service process to satisfy customers. Yet this satisfaction is crucial to both customers and service providers. (Blackman, 1985: 291)

The consumerist gap view of outcomes for clients is similar to the CS/D (Consumer Satisfaction/Dissatisfaction) model which focuses attention on the reactions of consumers to satisfying or dissatisfying purchases (Hunt, 1977). Thus, it has been argued that customers' experiences with any purchase give rise to outcomes for them varying from dissatisfaction to satisfaction. These are emotional responses, reflecting a divergence from expectations, as the following quotation indicates: 'The seeds of consumer satisfaction . . . are planted . . . during the prepurchase phase of the consumer decision process' (Wilkie, 1986: 558). Similarly, Engel, Blackwell and Miniard (1986: 155) defined satisfaction as 'a postconsumption evaluation that the chosen alternative is consistent with prior beliefs and expectations (with respect to it). . . . Dissatisfaction, of course, is that outcome when this confirmation does not take place.'

Service phases, episodes and events

Each type of tourism and hospitality service, for example car rental, hotel stays, retailing transactions or journeys by air, has its own delivery characteristics determined by the underlying technology of that service (Ingram, 2000; Ahmad, 2002). Noe (1999) has pointed out that the customer's focus of concern shifts to different attributes according to the phase of the service. In the case of journeys by air it has been found sufficient to distinguish five phases for the consumerist gap study (Table 3.2). However, one airline employs 180 categories for its internal analysis of service complaints.

Table 3.2 *Journeys by air: phases and events*

Phase	Example of event boosting satisfaction	Example of event decreasing satisfaction
Reservations	Suggestion offered to improve requested itinerary	Client has better knowledge of itinerary than staff member dealing with query
Check-in and arrival	Vegetarian meal request confirmed without asking	Prebooked seat not available Long wait for luggage
Boarding and disembarkation	Walk on to plane and find seat with no delay	Long queues in jetway
Meals	Problem with meal recognized and solution offered	Vegetarian meal not on board, client told off for not confirming request
Entertainment	Interesting film, good view and sound	Headphones do not work, film interrupted during transmission

Consumerist gap taxonomy for service encounter analysis

Analysis of passengers' reports of journeys by air indicates that an episode (journey) is understood by them as a series of events which have varying effects on their satisfaction, rather than as a simple, homogeneous experience. In the consumerist gap taxonomy an event is characterized by a change in the level of satisfaction reported, or it refers to separate elements in the service, such as the delivery of a meal tray, followed by beverage service (two events).

The term 'part-encounter' refers to a series of events which form part of the complete service. Typically, a part-encounter consists of the various events following a service interruption (such as a delay). Consequently, part-encounters are important in the client's overall evaluation of a service, although they are composed of separate events with varying levels of satisfaction. Part-encounters have both Type A and Type B characteristics, that is there are technical factors in the service delivery, and interaction occurs between clients and staff. Such face-to-face service encounters have been distinguished here from other events called 'mini-encounters' (Blackman, 1985), where the firm impacts on a client's consciousness through its advertising and other market place activities.

Each event in a service can be assigned to a specific service phase, although part-encounters can span more than one phase. Part-encounters are composed of a range of technical and service elements required to restore normal service after an interruption occurs. For example, in the event of a delay, announcements may be made, passenger comfort will be attended to, and a meal may be provided while Type A responses diagnose and repair the fault before the flight resumes. Many of these elements in the part-encounter will occur at an airport. Table 3.3 brings the terms described above together, and summarizes them.

Consumerist gap research methods

Much of the early consumerist gap research was carried out with a major airline which provided a series of observation flights, gave me opportunities to interview senior managers and also granted controlled access to its customer correspondence files. The series of observation flights enabled me to develop a database of flight experiences based on diaries of the events which were subsequently coded for analysis. The customer correspondence files provided a rich

Table 3.3 *Consumerist gap taxonomy for service encounter analysis*

Term	Definition
Satisfaction anticipated	The level of performance which the client had expected
Satisfaction experienced	The level of satisfaction actually experienced during the service, fluctuating event by event, and compared to the anticipated level
Acid test	Passed when the level of satisfaction matches that anticipated
Satisfaction boosters	Events which improve the client's satisfaction
Satisfaction depressants	Events, whether technical or service in origin, which reduce the client's level of satisfaction during service delivery
Technical events (Type A)	Occurrences attributed to the design or operation of a service
Service events (Type B)	Occurrences attributed to the performance of service tasks
Episode	The complete service such as a flight
Event	A discrete aspect of a service which influences clients' satisfaction
Service interruptions	Unplanned incidents noticed by the client, and resulting initially in depressed satisfaction levels (consumerist gaps). Managerial responses have the potential to restore (or worsen) satisfaction
Part-encounter	A set of connected events such as those occurring during the management of passenger satisfaction following a service interruption
Phase	Specific aspects of a service, such as reservations, meal service, etc.

Source: Laws (1992).

source of commentary documenting customers' experiences in their own words. A method was developed to code these, and they were incorporated in the database. Further data were obtained from focus group research with experienced travellers, including groups of academics interested in the project, and participation in the airline's professionally managed customer focus groups. The data were analysed using critical incident and content analysis techniques. At various stages they were summarized for discussion with airline managers who were able to provide operational insights into the events that had been observed and to discuss the processes used in response to particular situations.

The diary method and its limitations

The objective of the consumerist gap and service blueprinting approaches is to understand the customer's perspective of a service. The events during flights were initially recorded as simple diary entries, prior to coding and analysis (Laws and Ryan, 1992). Discussing visitor experiences at heritage sites, Masberg and Silverman (1996) noted that this requires an open-ended methodology which elicits insight into the varied and subjective nature of service experiences, rather than the more common survey methods which constrain respondents to categories of experience predetermined by the researcher. Visit diaries provide a means of studying the experiences of visitors in situ and have 'the power to discriminate between questions about settings and questions about people using the same data set' (ibid.: 20). Although diaries have been effective in researching tourists' responses to particular environments, they have been relatively neglected as a research tool in tourism.

The methodology has some of the features of participant observation. Jorgensen (1989) has noted that participant observation is most appropriate when concerned with human meanings and interactions from the insider's perspective, and the phenomenon is sufficiently limited in size and location to be studied as a case.

Just noticeable differences

The impact of any service event varies according to individual judgement. 'All experience, using the word in the widest possible sense, is either enjoyed or interpreted or both, and very little of it escapes some form of interpretation' (Hoch and Deighton, 1989). Accordingly, the observation diary records experiences during flights which resulted in discrete changes in satisfaction. The flight observation diary records six levels of changed satisfaction, whether boosting or depressing satisfaction compared to what had been expected. The 'mild' influences on satisfaction levels fall just outside subjectively acceptable bounds, whereas other events cause significant or extreme satisfaction or dissatisfaction. Engel, Blackwell and Miniard (1986: 156) argue that post purchase doubts are most probable when 'a certain threshold of dissonance motivated tension is surpassed'. Similarly, Weber's Law (discussed in Britt, 1975) proposed that a constant change is necessary for a given stimulus before the subject notices the change; however, the JND (just noticeable difference) varies between situations and between individuals. The just noticeable difference equates to the mild influences recorded in the observation diary as satisfaction fluctuated around the level anticipated. Approximately 65% of observations fell into the 'mild' category. This indicates that most clients experience their service as generally satisfactory. However, about a third of the service experiences recorded in my database were sufficiently annoying or pleasing for people to want to discuss them, and any of these could become the trigger for serious displeasure and complaint, or attract compliments for very satisfying service.

Content analysis theory

The consumerist gap report analysis method has similarities to content analysis. Carney (1972) has defined content analysis as a research technique for the objective, systematic and quantitative description of the content of selected communications, whether oral or written.

A distinction in the depth of analysis achievable by the consumerist gap method needs to be drawn between data generated by an observer and data obtained from others, either through unsolicited correspondence or focus groups. The problem relates to the structure, context and construction of meaning from communications. It is assumed in this study (although limits to the validity of the ensuing statement could be posited) that the observer has a clear and full understanding of his or her own observations. However, in the case of correspondence the exact meaning and importance of each aspect of the communication (and its relationship to the specific event or the general context of that traveller's experiences) is unknown. The focus group study and interviews with airline managers are an intermediate case, as discussion and questioning provided the researcher with opportunities to explore the meaning of their comments to those involved.

Carney (ibid.) has also pointed out that categories such as these are not clear cut, but are fuzzy categories. In the terminology of content analysis, the consumerist gap acid test really deals in fuzzy categories. At the heart of content analysis is the assigning of comments (words or phrases) to one of a few categories chosen by the researcher to encompass the main themes of interest. Similarly, the categories 'pass' or 'fail' to which all flights have been assigned are mutually exclusive. Scherl and Smithson (1987: 201) encountered a similar procedural problem during their content analysis of diaries recording Australian wilderness experiences.

> In virtually all cases coders are required to utilize their coding categories as if they were hard edged and mutually exclusive. Little attention has been paid to the possibility that a given datum might fit into more than one category simultaneously, or partly into one or more categories.

Critical incident techniques

In common with critical incident techniques, both ineffective and effective satisfaction management strategies were recorded in the consumerist gap observation diary, and analysed in the case studies, where they are classified as depressants or boosters. 'An incident is an observable activity that is complete enough in itself to allow inferences to be drawn and predictions to be made' (Flanagan, 1954: 331). In accordance with this definition, the length and content of each observation differs. A critical incident is defined as one which contributes to (or detracts from) the aims of the activity in some significant way. The approach has not received the attention it deserves, but it has been successfully adopted in studies by Stauss (1993) and Edvardsson and Strandvik (2000) among others.

Other researchers have suggested the analogy of a script (Abelson, 1976; Pine and Gilmore, 1999). Each consumer develops a script as he or she gains experience of a particular type of service. This is a composite memory of the various stages in a service, what they are required to do at each step, and how pleasing it is to them. It is against their own service script that they measure current experiences.

Both critical incident techniques and script-based analysis tend to focus on events which cause dissatisfaction. Psychologists define dissatisfaction as a state of cognitive or affective discomfort: the consumer has allocated some of his or her resources, spending money and time, and building up an anticipation of satisfaction; however, if his or her judgement of the service experienced is that it was not up to his or her standard, the customer will experience cognitive dissonance (Festinger, 1957). The consumer's response to any dissonant experience is an effort to correct the situation, or a determination to avoid it in the future. The correct managerial response has two components: to provide an acceptable remedy for the client, and to consider making changes to the service system, either in terms of a redesign or by improving the way it is delivered.

The researcher studying this type of situation needs 'sufficient detail so that it can later be analysed to give fair and unbiased results . . . [but] the customer's perception of this "moment of truth" is the central consideration when evaluating the quality of service' (Callan, 1998: 93). The critical incident method enables the 'researcher to get behind the attribute descriptions such as friendly staff and efficient staff to provide reasons for behaviour' (ibid.: 97). Bitner, Booms and Tetreault (1990) have confirmed the importance of the critical incident. In their view this often takes the form of an unsolicited and unscripted action by the service provider which makes or mars the customer experience.

Expectations of responses to service difficulties

CASE STUDY 3.1

Contrasting flight experiences:
non-availability of vegetarian meals

Figure 3.3 contrasts the different effects on my own satisfaction of two occasions when a vegetarian meal I had ordered was not loaded on to the flight. As I am a vegetarian, I always order a special meal when making my travel reservations: I confirm it with the airline a couple of days before departure, and again on checking in. Nevertheless, as in these two instances, the meal has sometimes not been available. In the diagram, meal episode 1

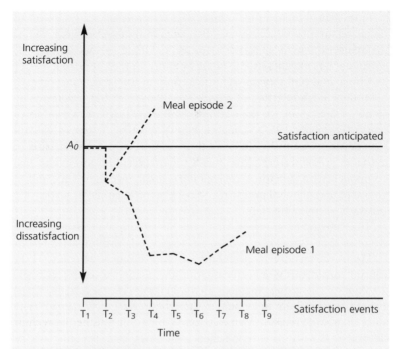

Figure 3.3 *Satisfaction outcomes of contrasting responses to similar problems*

traces the path of my declining state of satisfaction from the point where the stewardess passed me my meal tray and moved on. I had to press the attendant call button to summon her back as she was busy serving other passengers. When she eventually returned she told me curtly that there were no vegetarian meals at all on board, and informed me that I should have pre-ordered any special request. She moved away but I asked to see the Purser. She was holding the passenger manifest for the flight when she came to my seat, and showed it to me to prove that no vegetarian meal request was logged. She knelt down in the aisle and spent several minutes explaining correct procedure to order the meal, to the amusement of the passenger seated next to me. She took the offending dish away with her, and soon returned with an appetizing salad she had made up in the business class galley. The meal was satisfactory, but I remained dissatisfied with the service I had experienced.

On the second occasion the steward apologized for the absence of the meal I had ordered as soon as he reached my seat. He asked me to be patient, he would make sure that I had a satisfactory meal as soon as he had the time. A few minutes later he brought me a selection of cheeses and a plate of the vegetables they were serving in Business class, and gave me an extra portion of the wine served in economy in small bottles. As the path of meal episode 2 in Figure 3.3 indicates, I was quite satisfied with this service, and particularly the efficient and helpful way that the steward had taken the initiative in noticing and responding to my plight: the technical problem had been resolved by skilful service, before it became a crisis.

The foregoing example indicates that managers should not be afraid of situations where clients have some cause to complain. Most travellers are willing to make allowances for the vagaries of a journey, particularly in remote areas where the holiday experience takes on some features of an adventure, or when weather or technical problems are evidently the cause of a delay. However, knowledge of the concerns and problems which clients themselves experience, and an understanding of their reactions can assist in refining and improving the design of the service or the way in which it is delivered, including the company's responses to problem situations (Spreng, Gilbert and Mackoy, 1995; Tax, Brown and Chandrashekaran, 1998; de Ruyter and Wetzels, 2000; Leong, Kim and Ham, 2002; and Rafii and Kampas, 2002).

As Figure 3.4 shows, the way in which staff respond to problems can either attenuate or exacerbate the client's initial disappointments. Recognition of the problem, an apology and a solution usually restore satisfaction to normal levels, an extra gesture in recompense may boost satisfaction even higher, as shown by path A. In contrast path C is likely to deepen a client's dissatisfaction, as he or she has to initiate remedial action by complaining about a problem, and in the absence of an apology or compensation offers it is very unlikely that the result will be satisfactory, even if the original problem is corrected. Path B represents a number of possible intermediate cases where some aspects of the response to a problem are satisfactory while others are not.

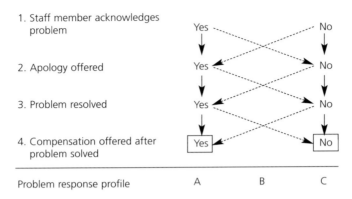

Figure 3.4 *Response profiles to service problems*

A synthesis of service experiences and service design

The implication of the consumerist gap approach and research by other authorities, notably Shostack, is that customer satisfaction can be managed. This is illustrated in Figure 3.5 where technical and service design aspects form the two poles on the horizontal axis. Another foundation of the consumerist gap concept is a recognition that the outcome of service events and interactions varies along a continuum ranging from extreme satisfaction to extreme dissatisfaction; this forms the vertical axis of the consumerist gap outcomes model.

Conclusion

The consumerist gap concept argues that each client anticipates a particular level of satisfaction from a service, but the satisfaction experienced may be more (or less) than anticipated. The pivotal idea in the concept is that satisfaction is individually defined, both in terms of what its determinants may be and in the extent to which satisfaction is experienced. Thus, the analysis sets a notional level with different values for each individual. A variety of factors can be identified which result in the varying expectations of each client participating in one service episode. These factors include their prior experience of similar episodes, any individual worries or concerns, and the company's marketing. The model highlights the process nature of tourism and hospitality services, and the complex interactions they entail between customers and staff which together contribute to the customer's overall experience and level of service satisfaction.

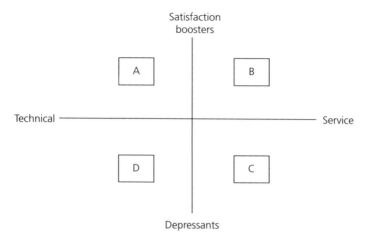

Figure 3.5 *Grid analysis of consumerist gap outcomes*

Quadrant **A** in the figure encompasses the conditions when a flight is operated efficiently at a technical level, proving comfortable, arriving on time and offering the passenger satisfying entertainment and meals as well as a pleasing standard of service from the staff.

Quadrant **B** describes a flight where any technical shortcomings such as delay or the non-delivery of a special meal request have been overcome by the effective responses of staff, or one where there were no difficulties, but service was particularly pleasing.

Quadrant **C** shows that it is not sufficient to restore the technical conditions of a service after a failure. If the response offends or provokes the passenger the result is seen in quadrant **C**, where the acid test has been failed, and the passenger is unwilling to return to that company.

Quadrant **D** results when technical factors do not match what the passenger had anticipated. As examples, the control of cabin pressure or temperature affects the way a passenger experiences a flight. Uncomfortable, broken or dirty seats are another example.

Overall, the model implies that managers who wish to satisfy their customers must provide both technical and service performance matching their expectations, that is, they must operate in both segment A and segment B to be effective.

CHAPTER 4

Tourism and hospitality service delivery systems

Introduction

This chapter is organized in two sections. The first section briefly discusses the Type A technical features of service operations while the second section introduces the techniques of service blueprinting and service mapping which provide frameworks for the deeper analysis in subsequent chapters of both the Type A and Type B features of a service.

Technical aspects of service systems

Service organizations need a range of physical and technical resources with which staff provide defined services to clients. The key choices for managers when designing services are the facilities, technology, and establishment of operating policies – that is, planning the service and controlling the way it is delivered – including the organization of operations to best meet market conditions. The strategic management of design therefore depends on a clear vision of what distinguishes one organization from competitors, and it includes communicating those differences, unequivocally, not only to its clients, but also to staff and service partners.

At one extreme, it could be argued that the physical setting for many tourist services is fixed. Tourist attractions such as historic castles and temples cannot be redesigned for the modern tourism industry; they are often inconvenient or difficult to move around in, and it is often impossible to see key features clearly as will be shown in the case study of Leeds Castle in Chapter 5. In contrast, the design of a new resort hotel or theme park can be based on concepts of its business potential, efficient operation, and a vision of its intended service style.

The designed service can be specified in terms of performance criteria for each element or component. In the case of airtravel, for example, the width, recline and leg-room of aircraft seats differ between classes of service and between airlines operating similar aircraft on the same routes. This is such an important decision factor for some passengers that there are now websites which provide up-to-date comparative tables. This type of service feature is relatively easy to control, although astute and experienced travellers will be aware that seats in particular cabin locations on one aircraft vary slightly in technical features. However, even these minor differences have resulted in consumer complaint and legal action when the advertised features are not provided. Recently, consumer concern has centred on DVT (deep vein thrombosis), a potentially life threatening condition which can arise from remaining in one position for a long period, and may be exacerbated by a cramped and unnatural posture. It should be noted that airlines are not free to operate as they see fit, but must comply with extensive and detailed international regulatory requirements as indicated in Case study 4.1.

CASE STUDY 4.1

Constraints to airline services

Airtravel is characterized by highly technical constraints within which the encounters between passengers and staff are carried out. The civil aviation industry is subject to a range of regulations, both national and international. In 1919 the International Airconvention of Paris established the basis of control for commercial operations, and the modern framework for regulation was laid down in the 1945 Chicago Convention. Two states were to negotiate between them the details of any bilateral agreement for mutual operations, including fares, total capacity and the division of that capacity between their two airlines. IATA (the International Air Transport Association) was to provide the commercial coordination for international fares.

Public concern over safety, noise and pollution is the justification for control over the servicing, staffing and operation of aircraft and related facilities. Passenger safety is also widely considered to be safeguarded by licensing and supervision. The regulation of air-routes and congestion at airports imposes further restrictions on all operators. The majority of technical and safety regulations are general, and apply to all passenger carriers. (In Britain they are contained in the Air Navigation Orders.) Variations between countries are very slight, and are based on a series of International Standards and Recommended Practices provided by ICAO (International Civil Aviation Organization) within the Convention on International Civil Aviation. Taken together, airlines face a series of technical rules known as 'non-economic regulations', shown in Table 4.1.

Traditionally, international air tariffs have been set by IATA, and must be approved by the governments concerned. Economic regulation of the international civil aviation industry is arranged under the Chicago Convention, which covers the exchange of air-traffic rights (freedoms of the air), the control of fares, and the control of frequencies and capacities. The result has been to constrain the ability of international airlines to take business decisions in two ways. Despite deregulation of the industry, airlines are not free to enter a market (route) at will; and secondly their revenue and growth is still limited by capacity controls, frequency rules or the imposed need to share a route with other airlines.

Table 4.1 *Non-economic regulations on airlines*

- The airworthiness of the aircraft
- The timing, nature and supervision of airframe, engine and other maintenance
- The numbers and qualifications of both flight and cabin crew; their training, licensing and schedules of work
- The ways in which aircraft are operated
- Standards dealing with civil aviation infrastructure

Style considerations

The form or design of a product is significant in several ways: 'First, in cluttered markets, product form is one way to gain consumer notice. Second, the exterior form of a product communicates information to consumers' (Block, 1995: 16). He noted that the aesthetic characteristics of more durable products can have a lasting effect on user and non-user alike as part of the sensory environment, arguing that design leads to a behavioural response. Spies, Hesse and Loesch (1997) showed that a favourable atmosphere can encourage the customer to spend longer in a retail store, buy more and feel more satisfied. Gardner (1987: 115) argued that mood can affect the way in which consumers process information. He pointed out that it 'is a transient state dependent on situational influences. Mood has direction and intensity, and is susceptible to rapid change.' The managerial perspective is discussed in Brown and Eisenhardt (1995) and by Dwyer, Murray and Mott (1998), who also evaluate a continuous improvement approach.

Another example of how regulations impact on an airline's service brand style is the announcement by one major American carrier in its October 1999 frequent flyer newsletter that preflight welcoming drinks served to business and first class passengers would in future have to be presented in paper cups to comply with new FAA safety regulations. This airline, like many of its competitors, had long made a point of including in its advertising an array of fine linen, tableware and wines served to its premium class passengers. The new paper cup service may be contrasted with one note in my observation diary, recorded during a flight on the same airline a few years earlier: 'As soon as most were seated, papers, orange juice and champagne (Pol Roger) were offered to business passengers, presented in attractive crystal glasses as the standard welcome message was broadcast.'

Airlines are discussed in some detail here because of my inherent interest in the industry, because airtransport is a key factor in the development of much of the tourism industry, and because the unique isolation of passengers and staff within a very high-technology environment highlights the critical factors influencing clients' satisfaction outcomes. The major technical constraint (Type A) on in-flight service is the detailed design of the aircraft fuselage and its ancillary equipment for catering, entertainment and comfort. A case study summarized here shows how the planning of aircraft cabins is regarded as a significant factor by carriers in differentiating their services.

CASE STUDY 4.2

Service differentiation through cabin design

Discussing a note in the 1982/83 report that SAS had not added a single plane to its fleet that year, Jan Carlzon, SAS president, said: 'What we were really looking for was what we called the "Passenger Pleasing Plane", or the "Three P Plane". We needed a 150-seat plane with an innovative passenger compartment including such enhancements as:

- more space to store hand luggage
- wider twin aisles for easier mobility
- wider doors
- reduced cabin noise
- no middle seats

A nine-point scale was used to assess passengers' ratings for existing seating comfort, seat width and leg-room. A score of −1 indicated a very high level of dissatisfaction, while +1 indicated very high satisfaction levels. This information was correlated with other data collected in the survey to specify the exact seat and conditions around that passenger. Passengers seated between two others gave an overall rating of −.95; those between a passenger and an aisle −.38; those between another passenger and a window −.25; and those between an aisle and an empty seat 0. The most preferred seat was that between a window and an empty seat, with a positive rating of .25. SAS decided to configure its new international fleet without middle seats in business class. The 767 was the only plane which enabled them to do that economically.'

Based on Mathieson (1988)

In the airline industry, one of the most immediately recognizable designs was Concorde. Due to the very high fares charged for supersonic flight and the small number of Concordes flying, operated by Air France and British Airways, few travellers had the opportunity to fly in it. However, it was quite often seen in a number of airports and on several occasions I heard captains of other aircraft direct their passengers' attention to a Concorde parked nearby at the Heathrow terminal. Shortly after it was introduced into service one captain announced 'we'll pass it mid-Atlantic'. He paused, then added gleefully, 'on its way back!'*

Architectural spaces and retail atmospherics are known to influence buyer behaviour when shopping. A familiar example is the 'muzak' played in large stores and shopping centres, or the policy of locating an instore bakery at the rear of a supermarket in order to entice customers towards the aroma of freshly baked bread, so that they have to pass through the aisles of canned, bottled and packaged goods, hopefully adding more items to their shopping trolleys than they had planned to.

The effects on consumers of design features can be considered along an approach–avoidance continuum. Some tourism icons such as the Eiffel Tower or the exclusive resort of Monaco attract people through their pleasing form, providing what Bitner (1992) has called a 'servicescape' encompassing the service environment layout, ambient conditions and physical features. In contrast, there are other examples where careless design or shoddy construction have become threats to the continuing success of local tourism enterprises. This is characteristic of some unplanned resorts around the Mediterranean, developed by speculators in response to the tourism boom of the 1960s and 1970s. Many have begun to implement policies to pull down the worst buildings, redesign the resort layout and improve the standards of service they offer (Laws and Cooper, 1998). This point is considered further in a discussion of pricing tourism services in a later chapter, but it is relevant here because there seems to be an innate preference for orderly, unified designs.

Many companies acknowledge the contribution which design can make to the success of their service, but the issue is how to identify what constitutes effective design. A criticism of much market research is that it is mainly an analysis of past behaviour, or projections based on that, and therefore is not relevant to the creation of innovatory service concepts. Decisions about the optimal design are aided by data to help define the service process, its problems and capabilities. Table 4.2 lists five factors to consider when developing

---

* In early 2003 the two airlines operating Concorde fleets, BA and Air France, both announced that they would be 'retiring' them later in the year. Richard Branson declared that he would try to acquire them for Virgin Atlantic (Done, 2003), but all Concordes have now been withdrawn from service.

the physical layout of a service. The criteria for effective design also need to be re-evaluated periodically in the context of shifts in technology and cultural variables.

Table 4.2 *Factors to consider when developing the physical layout of a service*

- capacity
- time taken
- quality yields
- values
- cost build-ups.

Based on Schmenner (1995)

Performance criteria

It is a basic practice for managers to specify the technical performance goals for the main events in a service delivery system. A familiar example is the target of answering the office telephone before it has rung more than a given number of times, or of delivering a burger within a stated number of minutes of ordering it. Transport companies publicize the proportion of their 'on-time' arrivals, and airlines aim to open the plane's doors within two minutes of 'engines-off'. It is common for companies to feature good performance on these criteria in advertising, as an extension to benchmarking against competitors (Gilbert and Pahizgari, 2000; Pyo, 2002). However, many goals of this type are actually dependent on the way staff perform their roles. Locke and Schweiger (1979) identified eight characteristics of effective programmes dependent on staff, summarized in Table 4.3.

Table 4.3 *Effective performance targets*

- specific
- accepted
- cover important job dimensions
- reviewable
- provide appropriate feedback
- measurable
- challenging
- attainable

Based on Locke and Schweiger (1979)

Design errors

If a fault is built into a system its users have to cope with the resultant problems on a regular basis. Deming (1982) regards commonly
occurring faults as responsible for over 90% of problems, while the
remainder are due to special factors such as carelessness, lack of
knowledge or bad temper. Similarly, Crosby (1984) argues that from
70% to 90% of all quality problems are repetitive, and built into the
process. This strongly points to the benefits of designing quality into
the service development process, as recommended by Juran (1982).

The first of the following two case studies illustrates technical
weaknesses in the physical features within which a service is
provided. This can be contrasted with the problem resulting from a
lack of understanding of travellers' motivations and interests,
outlined in Case study 4.4.

CASE STUDY 4.3

A new ticket hall

One of London's mainline railway station booking offices illustrates the interplay between two main components of tourism: its
technical or physical features, and the service elements. This
booking hall is long with plenty of booking windows, but shallow
so few people can queue at each window at any one time. It is
located off the main concourse underneath an overhanging
office structure supported on heavy pillars, each one approximately a metre wide. These pillars have two detrimental effects
on the experience of queuing for tickets, and the general
problems which their presence imposes is exacerbated by a
service design flaw. Although there are as many as 14 sales
windows open in peak periods, each has a separate queue line.
The pillars confuse customers because their placement relative to
the sales windows causes queues to slant across the waiting area,
or to have a pronounced bend after about eight customers line
up. Newcomers are therefore unsure which queue is the shortest,
while people already in line can be seen to become uncertain,
and sometimes switch between queues. This is exacerbated by
some people's urgent need to purchase tickets for a train about
to depart. Tickets can be purchased on board the train, but the

operating companies impose a penalty on passengers travelling without a valid ticket in the form of a £10.00 surcharge.

Several automatic ticket machines have been located outside the booking hall. This solution has not proved particularly successful because the queues at busy times run past the machines, causing disputes between those waiting in the lines and others pushing past to get to the machines. Another problem is that the majority of automatic machines only sell tickets to local suburban stations, while it seems from observation that the majority of people queuing for tickets are travelling to the long distance stations served from the station. Some of the automatic ticket machines can be used for these destinations, but most customers queue, either because they prefer individual advice, including information on departure times and platforms, or they are simply unaware that they could purchase tickets for any journey from the appropriate automatic machine.

Another service which many travellers require is information; this is provided at a separate, although adjacent, location. Outside the information office is a set of racks from which travellers can select (and take free of charge) local timetables for some of the lines served from the station. However, the selection often seems arbitrary, and many other timetables are only available 'on request' from the information office staff. Inside the information office (and in contrast to the ticket office), a roped line has been set up for people to queue beside, the available staff serving whichever customer has reached the head of the queue.

CASE STUDY 4.4

Managing tourists' activities in China

The activities or excursions included in a tourism holiday package are normally selected to meet their interests, but when the People's Republic of China first began to accept foreign visitors, their itineraries were carefully controlled and included features which few enjoyed, while what they wanted to do was often forbidden. One Chinese guide recorded his frustration at these conditions: 'The first visitors to China encountered a packed programme of early morning starts, and gruelling itineraries of visits to schools, factories and farms to demonstrate the modern achievements of Chinese people. There was little opportunity to do your own thing, wander at will or even to influence the itinerary, and much of China was closed to visitors . . . in Sichuan we were to find it difficult to persuade the driver to stop beside the road to watch the second rice planting of the year, and buffalo ploughing the fields . . . [they] expressed surprise at our interest on such "ordinary" scenes of life. And down the road in Leshan . . . as I talked to a local boat owner repairing nets by the river he asked in bewildering and genuine concern, "why do you show these people our old boats? Take them to see our modern buildings." He pointed to a block of flats!' (Wang, 1991: 8).

Since then, China has become much more open to tourists, and its service style is quite consistent with Western expectations. Its policies of attracting overseas tourists have been so successful that in 2000 it was ranked fifth by number of arrivals, with 31 million visitors (WTO, 2002), and it is rapidly becoming a major source market of international tourists (Pan and Laws, 2001).

Service blueprinting

The examples given previously have shown that tourism services are complex processes involving the interaction of technology, staff and customers: it is now recognized that the outcomes of service systems depend in large part on the way they are designed. It was shown in Chapter 1 how Lynn Shostack, then Director of an American bank, was critical of poor service design, of managers who failed to recognize responsibility for defining what it actually is that their organization provides. She advocated service blueprinting as a way of analysing an existing service, gaining a customer perspective on it, and identifying potential problem areas, the failpoints or areas of weakness which it was critical for managers to address. The technique has been extended and further refined, and now embraces service mapping and perceptual service mapping. The purpose of these techniques is essentially the same: to try to understand what customers expect from a service, the sequence of events they experience during a service, and how the underlying technology contributes to their satisfaction. The customer's perspective can be presented as a flow chart, and then matched to the processes involved in delivering the service, even though many of these are invisible to the customer. Mismatches become the focus of investigation, to identify causes, and evaluate the cost of potential consequences and of remedial action. It is the designed service which encapsulates the organization's vision of its distinctive offering, and this is the basis for communication between the organization's managers and its customers, staff and suppliers.

The value of service blueprinting is that the many interactions between clients and the providers of complex services can be identified in the underlying technical design. Blueprinting a service in this way shows that in many instances little of the service is actually visible to the consumer. Shostack called this phenomenon 'the service iceberg'. The implication for service managers is that all aspects of the service design have to be managed from the perspective of how they impinge on customers' experiences. Particular attention should be paid to the invisible processes which consumers are unaware of, because these are the basis for the service and can cause success or failure. (This is somewhat similar to the dichotomy between front and back region performances originally distinguished by Erving Goffman, 1959.)

Berkely (1996: 152) recommends blueprinting as 'one of the most sophisticated and promising approaches to service design . . . [it] provides service designers with a way to visualise service processes and to identify opportunities for improvement'. Traditionally, a blueprint is an ordered technical drawing in which the symbols represent instructions to technicians which they use as a template in manufacturing processes, or in wiring electrical circuitry.

The basic service blueprint should have three main features (Shostack, 1984). It must incorporate within the design a time dimension, enabling the researcher to follow the customer's progress through the service delivery process. Secondly, it should show the main functions which together comprise the service, and show their interconnectedness. Figure 4.1 follows Shostack's original blueprinting convention with a single horizontal dividing line to distinguish the front-of-house events visible to clients from those which occur offstage and are invisible to them, but which underpin service delivery.

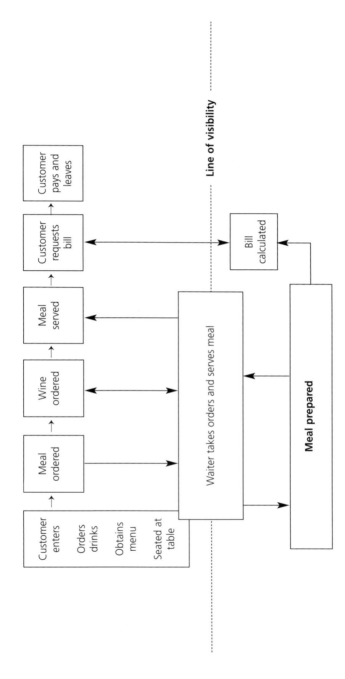

Figure 4.1 *Basic restaurant service blueprint*

Shostack argued that the third feature of a blueprint is that it should incorporate performance standards for each stage of the process. This introduces a further feature of service blueprints: they can be used to identify failpoints, the parts of a service which are most likely to cause errors (George and Gibson, 1988). This feature provides the diagnostic capability of the service blueprinting method employed in this book.

Mapping tourism services

Service blueprinting can be used when designing a new service, as this is its managers' main opportunity to determine the characteristics of the service offered to customers. It is also a useful methodology to investigate the issues confronting managers of an established service delivery process, assisting in examining the potential for improvements to services or facilities through examining customers' evaluations of each step of the service process (Berkely, 1996; Botschen, Bstieler and Woodside, 1996). Lovelock (1994) has described how a hospital in Boston evaluated its patients' experiences of the service aspects of the hospital through flowcharting methods. The insights which resulted provided essential inputs into a design for the physical layout of new facilities. However, the option of physical redevelopment is not often available to tourism managers, whose service design is constrained within the 'hard' structure of a hotel building or aircraft fuselage and who must usually seek improvements to the 'soft' aspects of the service. The important issue of the financial benefits to the firm of implementing particular design enhancements in comparison with the costs of doing so are considered later.

Service mapping is distinguished from service blueprinting notably by the increased levels of delivery system analysis it offers. Service maps add complexity back into the basic blueprinting concept, with additional information layers (or levels) which record additional factors such as the interactions between customer and contact staff, between contact staff and support staff, and between staff and managers, who may be remote from the service delivery location.

Service mapping has been described as a process which

visually defines a service system, displaying each sub-process within the sequence. . . . The map should revolve around the explicit actions the customer takes to receive the service. . . . The specific contacts the customer has with contact personnel are mapped, as are the internal services (invisible to the customer) that support contact services. (Berry, 1995: 86)

Shostack and Kingman-Brundage (1991) have together generalized the management procedures needed for service development, emphasizing the iterative nature of defining services, analysing the data, synthesis and drawing conclusions. Their joint view is that blueprinting and its developments contribute to the master design of the service and facilitate improvement and redesign as a result of continually increasing knowledge. Commenting on this, Gummesson (1991: 191) noted: 'The strengths of the procedural models . . . is . . . that they directly emanate from empirical material on service development where blueprinting was applied. It is in part inductive research and an application of grounded theory.'

Since each of the events in a service is actually composed of many steps (Berkely, 1996), the amount of detail in service designs can be overwhelming: Schmenner (1995) identified 19 separate steps involved in the write-up of an auto repair order, itself shown as one event in a blueprint. However, it should be evident that a complete specification of kitchen procedures is essential to management when setting up or improving a catering operation!

Development of service blueprinting

The basic blueprint model can be developed in two significant ways: by including consideration of the pre and post service as well as the core events, and by a zone within which the service technology is visible to a greater or lesser extent. The service literature suggests that a customer experiences the service as a series of events occurring in several phases. Lalonde and Zinzser (1976) distinguished three phases: pre-transaction, transaction and post-transaction. From the point of view of the outcomes of the service system, the significance of the pre-transaction phase is that these events can influence the way a customer approaches the core service. For example, a difficult journey to the airport is quite a common experience for travellers, and there is little that the airline can do to alleviate a passenger's stress and concern that he or she might miss the flight. In less difficult conditions, the customer might hardly be aware of the journey to the airport, a state of mindlessness which Moscardo (1999) has described in some detail, but when problems arise the customer's awareness is heightened. The customer actively evaluates each phase of the service and his or her overall satisfaction with it, against what had been anticipated. If the customer is in a bad mood when he first has contact with the service provider, staff are confronted with the need to calm him down to make him receptive to the service process. This may partly explain the offer by some airlines of a complimentary limousine service between home or office and airport for premium class passengers as an enhancement to the core flight service.

The second major refinement to service blueprinting recognizes that the range of tasks which constitute a service vary in the degree to which they are visible to clients, suggesting a zone of visibility rather than a line clearly delineating aspects of the service which customers see from others which are not at all visible to them. These points are illustrated in Figure 4.2 and have the potential to open up analysis of the ways in which customers participate in various aspects of the service, as will be demonstrated next.

	Pre-transaction	Core service delivery and consumption	Post-transaction
Customer experiences			
Service encounters			
Technical service activities			

Figure 4.2 *The nine cells of a full blueprint*

Service blueprinting as a research tool

By providing a structured way to investigate the nature of service design and service interactions, the operational distinctions between different types of services (for example, restaurant, hotel, heritage site visit or travel services) can be investigated and compared in terms of general management and service management theories. Case study 4.5 shows how blueprinting was used in a comparative investigation of two styles of service run in parallel by a small catering company. In this example, a group of students carried out much of the research as part of their honours degree course.

CASE STUDY 4.5

Blueprinting analysis of a pizza restaurant and delivery service

The blueprints presented in Figures 4.3 and 4.4 depict the two services offered by an independent pizza business combining a restaurant and takeaway/delivery service. The owner's objective was to provide high quality individually prepared pizzas for clients eating in the 25-seat restaurant, and for those ordering home delivery. The business is located near the campus of a large university.

Several family members took turns in preparing the bills, taking payments and supervising the restaurant and dispatch activities. The owner of this pizza company himself prepared the pizza dough in batches and supervised his kitchen teams. These were part timers (mainly catering students), and he employed several students as cooks and combined telephone order takers, packers, and waiters. Other students were employed to deliver the pizzas using their own motor cycles. Furthermore, because of its location, many of its patrons for both the delivery service and restaurant meals were students. The preponderance of students among the staff and clients of the business suggests that word of mouth recommendation might be significant, and that the potential for critical comment following any negative experiences could be potentially damaging.

Pizzas were prepared and baked individually to order for both restaurant and home delivery order clients, and most clients regarded the pizzas as being very satisfying to eat. However, the owner was aware that both types of clients experienced a number of problems, as discussed below, and so he agreed to participate in an academic blueprinting exercise with the proviso that his company would not be identifiable in any publication.

A group of students in the final year of an honours degree course were introduced to the blueprinting method. They were

asked to purchase a meal in the restaurant and to order a delivered pizza, keeping a diary of their experiences. Each student also
interviewed a number of fellow students – either part-time staff
or customers of the pizza restaurant and the pizza delivery service
– to explore the most memorable aspects of the service, high-
lighting both good and bad experiences and accounting in their
own terms for these events.

The two blueprints presented and discussed below summarize
those produced by the students. They have been simplified for
presentation and discussion here, following a technique advocated by Ramaswamy (1996). The students' original work had
identified some 40 elements in the service delivery systems, and
discussed some two dozen failpoints. The blueprints presented
here also benefited from further discussion and clarification with
the pizza company's owner. The students' accounts of reported
incidents provided the basis for the failpoints indicated in the
service blueprints and discussed in the text which follows.

The restaurant service blueprint
Following the conventions outlined above, the restaurant service
blueprint in Figure 4.3 is divided into three horizontal zones and
three vertical sections. The vertical dotted lines separate the three
service phases, pre-service (or attachment, when the customer
telephones to make a booking), the core service (during which
the meal is consumed), and the detachment phase (when the bill
is settled, the customer leaves, and subsequently reflects on his or
her experience, evaluating it as satisfactory or not). The horizontal dotted lines separate the features of the service. The upper
section can be understood as the customer's conceptual flow
chart of the sequence of events he or she is likely to experience
during the service episode. The central zone of visibility records
the elements of the service delivery system when the customer
interacts with staff, while the area beneath this plots the range of
activities and events which are required to create the service. The
vertical and horizontal areas of the blueprint are linked by
customer-contact staff in the performance of their roles in delivering service to the customer. The blueprint is annotated with
failpoints numbered FP 1.1–1.6 which are discussed in the text
below.

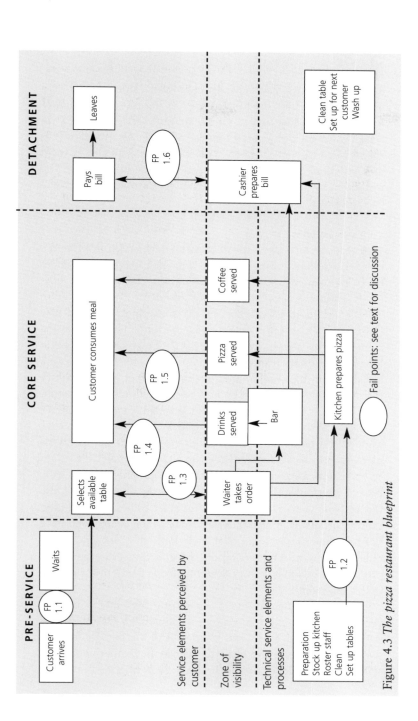

Figure 4.3 *The pizza restaurant blueprint*

Pre-service phase

Restaurant clients may experience problems prior to the core service of consuming their pizzas (FP 1.1). Because the restaurant is small, and offers only a simple style of service, there is no booking system. The limited number of tables often means that clients have to wait; however, the few chairs available to them are also used by delivery riders waiting for instructions. The restaurant owner believed that he had lost customers under these circumstances.

Core service phase

The consumption phase is the main part of any service, in which the client experiences the tangible and intangible service, and judges his or her experiences against expectations. As the service blueprints indicate, a variety of failpoints may occur. The owner shops daily in the local markets for the pizza toppings, choosing only fresh, attractive goods. Consequently, the range indicated on the menus is not always available (FP 1.2) but, conversely, other toppings are often offered as 'specials'. These are marked up on a blackboard in the waiting area of the restaurant, visible both to clients and to the telephone order takers. Restaurant clients benefit from a discussion with their waiter if an item is not available (FP 1.3). As soon as a pizza is ordered, a member of the kitchen crew spins out the dough for the crust, adds the toppings and places the pizza into any available oven space on a long wooden ladle.

The waiter also serves drinks. These are obtained (FP 1.4) from the bar which is controlled by a relative of the owner, who is also the cashier. A delay in serving after-meal drinks often results, causing problems in peak business hours when clients who have finished their pizzas linger over their wine, thus delaying subsequent customers. (The serving of coffee further exacerbates this problem, although it has not been flagged as a potential failpoint in this blueprint.)

When a member of the kitchen crew sees that a pizza is cooked, he or she places it on to a large wooden platter, slices it with a large roller blade, and matches it to the original order. A waiter then presents the pizza to the clients, bringing domestic-style knives and forks which are wrapped in brightly patterned, heavy paper napkins. However, pizzas are sometimes mismatched to their order specification (FP 1.5), either because an item is unavailable, or because of a mistake. When a client notices this and complains to the waiter, the company's standard response is for the waiter to apologize, and to offer complimentary coffee to the party. This has usually resulted in a satisfactory outcome.

Detachment phase

The cashier's position is adjacent to the exit, and after completing consumption of the core service, the customer settles his or her bill and departs (FP 1.6). This phase of service also presents problems: these arise from the other roles of the cashier, which were previously mentioned (as bar tender and as restaurant manager) and more particularly because clients sometimes complain that there are discrepancies on the bill. This is usually caused by substitution of toppings for a pizza, and is usually resolved quickly and quietly. The cashier also takes pride in assisting clients' departure by retrieving coats, phoning for a taxi, or bidding them farewell, thus contributing to their overall positive evaluation of the service.

The pizza delivery service blueprint

In contrast with the restaurant service blueprint, the blueprint for pizza delivery service (Figure 4.4) follows Shostack's (1981) original approach, being divided into only two sections by a horizontal line of visibility. Failpoints in the delivery service blueprint are numbered FP 2.1–2.9. The simple menus distributed may have been lost by potential clients who therefore never contact the company (FP 2.1). The delivery customer's first association with the service begins some time before the meal, when telephoning to place an order. Subsequently, the customer awaits delivery. Both of these can result in disappointment. In fact, the service sometimes fails at these points, either due to lack of response to the phone call (FP 2.2), or because customers become frustrated by an overlong wait (FP 2.9). As a consequence of multiple roles necessitated by the small business environment, the person assigned to take telephoned orders is often engaged in taking orders from restaurant clients, with the result that potential delivery clients abandon their call. Similarly, the owner stated that there have been examples of a customer refusing to accept delivery of a pizza in extreme cases of delay.

The general model of service blueprinting assumes that detachment is the culmination of a service, but the home-delivered pizza service does not follow this logical sequence: the customer's final interaction with the company, accepting delivery and paying for the pizza (FP 2.9), is actually followed by the core consumption phase. This is significant because there are no further opportunities for the company to remedy any problems easily, such as a pizza made with incorrect ingredients. Such occurrences sometimes cause the customer to complain formally, when the company's response is usually to provide the com-plainant with a coded reference number entitling a discount off a future pizza order. However, the interviews with students indicate that some do not complain to the company, but they often grumble to colleagues about any poor service experienced. The significance of this behaviour is discussed below.

Discussion of the delivery service blueprint

Any of the elements in a service delivery system has the potential to cause problems, but difficulties are more likely to occur with certain aspects of a given service operation. Table 4.4 (p. 70) elab-orates on the causes of, and suggests possible remedies to, the main failpoints identified in Figure 4.4. The remedies proposed were discussed with the pizza company owner, to evaluate their feasibility and costs of implementation, but these details, and the owner's views of operational priorities, are not discussed further.

Further discussion

Comparison of the two blueprints revealed that the key weakness was the reduced number of interactions with staff experienced by the delivered-pizza customers. This had the effect of reducing the opportunities to resolve technical or service problems as they arose. Consequently, difficulties which were easy to remedy in the higher contact restaurant service more often resulted in dissatis-faction for customers who had their pizzas delivered.

Based on Laws (2001)

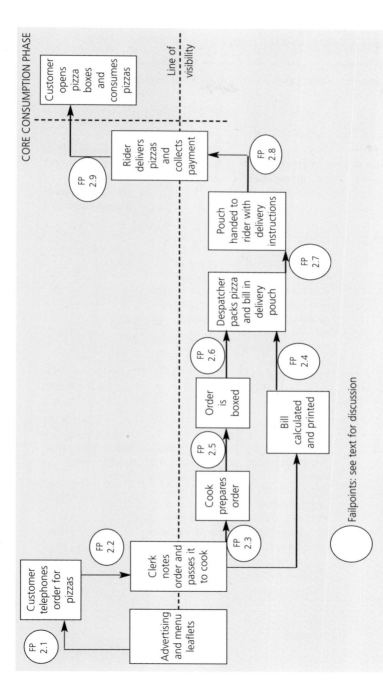

Figure 4.4 The pizza delivery blueprint

Table 4.4 *Pizza delivery service analysis*

Failpoint	Description	Suggested remedial action	
		Service design	Resource implication
2.1	Loss of menu by potential delivered-pizza customer.	Make menu more present-able.	Improve printing and/or quality of paper. Distribute menus more frequently.
2.2	Delay in answering phone, or customer put on hold. Customer not informed of items unavailable, or not offered additional items to enhance meal ordered. Clerk makes errors in recording order, or customer's address.	Simplify ordering procedure. Improved design of forms to maximize accuracy.	Additional staffing. Training in order taking.
2.3	Delay due to pro-cessing previous orders. Cook misreads order, overlooks an item or substitutes for something unavailable.	Clearer order forms and more legible writing. Substitution, when needed, should be confirmed with client.	Additional cooks and/or ovens needed.
2.4	Mistakes in listing or costing items ordered. Substitutions not recorded.	Procedure required to check items on bill against pizzas packed.	

Figure 4.4 *continued*

Failpoint	Description	Suggested remedial action	
		Service design	**Resource implication**
2.5	Damage to pizza when inserting it in box.		Improved box needed. Train cooks to take more care.
2.6	Wrong pizza loaded into pouch with client's address.	Recheck pizza against delivery note.	
2.7	Delayed delivery.	Ensure they return to base promptly after each delivery.	Recruit more delivery riders.
2.8	Difficulty in contacting client, problems in collecting payment.	Check address carefully with client when taking order. Obtain prior authorization for credit card payments.	Provide delivery riders with more change for large denomination notes.
2.9	Contents found to be not as ordered when client opens pizza boxes, pizzas cold or damaged.	Strengthen checks at failpoints 2.2, 2.3, and 2.7.	Speed up production and delivery procedures. Improve packaging.

Perceptual blueprinting

Another type of blueprint was developed by Senior and Akehurst (1992), organized around trying to understand customers' perceptions of a service system, or their experiences of using it. This approach emphasizes the service events from the customers' perspectives and is based on interviews, focus groups and participant observation techniques. It is used by researchers interested in service interactions and customer attitudes, and places less detailed emphasis on the complex variety of tasks needed to deliver a service.

Whereas operations research is concerned with physically structured problems, soft systems methodology and perceptual blueprinting look at

> unstructured problem situations in which unpredictable human behaviour is a determining influence on the success or failure of a system. . . . Systems are coexisting technical and social systems which cannot be treated in isolation, yet design efforts often concentrate so much on the hard technical aspects that they neglect the soft social and less mechanical aspects. (Ibid.: 8).

This is particularly helpful, because it is widely accepted that customers' perceptions of service events differ, and that individual quality judgements are based on the divergence of the service experiences from service anticipated. It takes on some of the characteristics of iterative or action research, in which managers are interrogated about the operational meaning (and validity) of their clients' commentary on the existing service delivery system. A subsequent phase explores the setting of managerial priorities and the remedial action to be taken in redressing the failpoints identified earlier.

Figure 4.5 (pp. 74–75) is a perceptual map of an inclusive holiday. The tourist experiences a series of events such as the flight, the hotel and so on shown by the boxes 1–11 in the upper section. These extend vertically across the line of visibility into the zone of visibility in the form of a series of service encounters. A number of failpoints which might occur are noted below the main service map, with short examples. Research for a tour operator to determine what aspects of their holiday clients considered the company responsible for elicited the typical responses shown in the bottom row of Figure 4.5. Invisible to the client, the company carries out a sequence of technical tasks such as contracting for the flights.

As Figure 4.6 indicates, these may span a long period of time prior to the customer's holiday taking place. During the interval between booking a holiday and embarking on it, the client's expectations may intensify, or he or she may notice a similar holiday being offered for a lower price, or an alternative destination may be promoted. Therefore, it is quite possible that the client's level of expectations (A_0 in the consumerist gap model; see Figure 3.2 on page 34) may be lower or higher when the holiday starts compared with when the booking was made.

Implications for organizational change

A service blueprint conceptualizes the geography of a service, but the way it has been configured is not a given in the sense that a map of a town locates the spatial relationships of geographically fixed places. Many of the events which comprise a service could be redesigned or rescheduled to avoid problem areas such as bottlenecks which result from an inappropriate layout or schedule for the process.

It can be seen from this that blueprinting or mapping a service has implications for the way that it is managed, not least because the approach makes the way a service works more transparent. 'Service systems blueprints simplify service complexities by displaying the operation of existing systems' (Kingman-Brundage, 1989: 30). This transparency and simplification enables management to concentrate on areas which are the most likely to cause poor service delivery and to make sensible decisions in relation to service by observing the service procedures. This also applies to the people who deliver the service. Therefore, Schmenner (1995: 43) notes that 'people should be free to question why some things are done as they are'.

Davis (1989: 11–13) suggests that the managerial implementation of blueprinting solutions depends on four approaches which extend its scope into the functioning organization:

- *enable* (determine customers needs and coordinate service delivery);
- *empower* (establish what needs to be done to enable the customer to receive appropriate service delivery);
- *monitor* (analyse the way in which service is conducted);
- *mentor* (help service delivery staff to deliver better service).

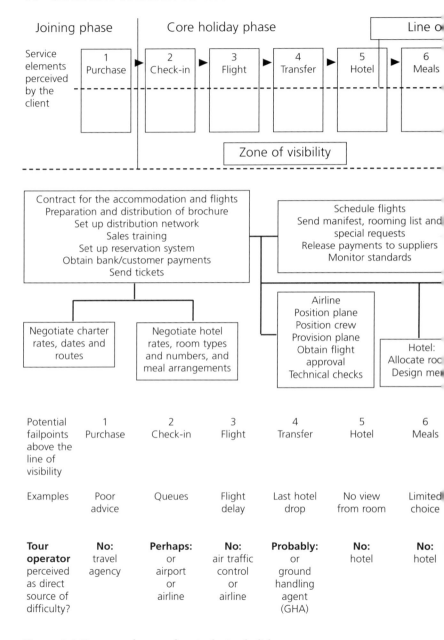

Figure 4.5 *Perceptual map of an inclusive holiday*

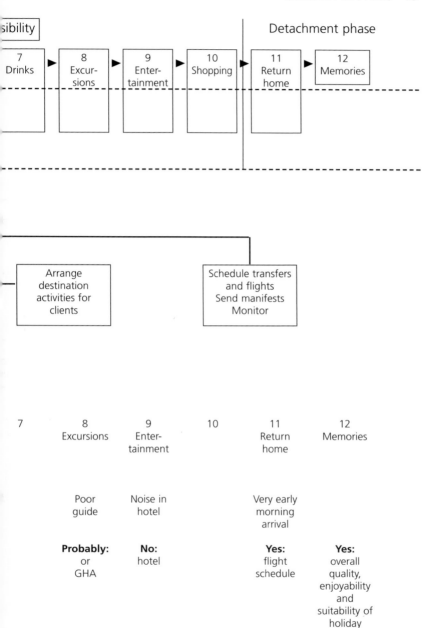

sibility				Detachment phase	
7 Drinks	8 Excur- sions	9 Enter- tainment	10 Shopping	11 Return home	12 Memories

Arrange destination activities for clients

Schedule transfers and flights
Send manifests
Monitor

7	8 Excursions	9 Enter- tainment	10	11 Return home	12 Memories
	Poor guide	Noise in hotel		Very early morning arrival	
	Probably: or GHA	**No:** hotel		**Yes:** flight schedule	**Yes:** overall quality, enjoyability and suitability of holiday

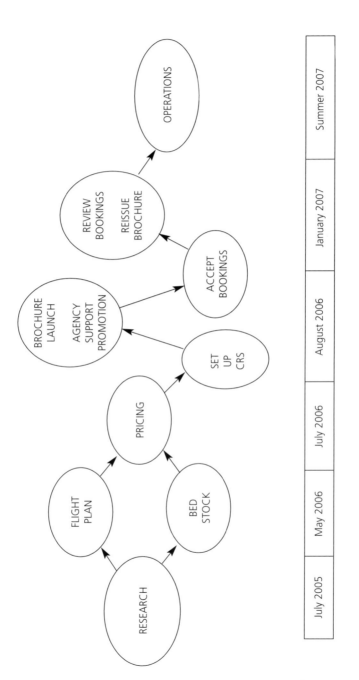

| July 2005 | May 2006 | July 2006 | August 2006 | January 2007 | Summer 2007 |

Figure 4.6 *Managerial planning for an inclusive holiday*

The foundations for an understanding of service quality are based on 'a balance between human input and technology, between costs and income, and finally between quality and productivity' (Gummesson, 1991: 40). This approach is more than a shift in focus; it represents a new way of thinking and can be said to be a new paradigm as it is dependent on a new style of management and the fostering of an organizational climate which actively supports the philosophy of service quality as a major company objective. In particular, it suggests the need to empower customer-contact staff, and to do so by focusing the organization's resources and its managers' skills on satisfying (legitimate) customer expectations (Lashley, 1997; Hjalager, 2001). Achieving this requires the organization to encourage a culture of continuing quality improvements. These issues are examined in more depth in a later chapter. The consumerist gap approach helps us to understand the way that customers experience the technical and service aspects while the blueprinting method relates customer perceptions of the underlying and often invisible service processes.

Conclusion

Service blueprint and service mapping approaches highlight the series of relationships between customers, service contact staff and the technical elements of the service defined by the sequence of events in a complete service episode. Blueprints are communications tools useful to managers when designing new services because it can be seen whether all the elements and processes are set out logically. They are also helpful when deciding how to improve existing services. They 'provide managers with valuable insights into where their customers believe that service is failing, although in itself it is not able to prioritise their impacts, or evaluate alternative methods and costs of remedial actions' (Laws, 1997: 54). They are also useful when developing a new service, as features which have the potential to cause problems can be spotted and eliminated before they occur.

The key benefit which comes from blueprinting is the potential to improve service. Johnston (1999) notes that many restaurants have seemingly adapted the technique, seeking the advantage of preconceived failpoints, so that mistakes in the service process can be prevented from happening. The blueprint can demonstrate where processes create value for customers, keeping them the focal point of service delivery. Overall, blueprints and service maps 'present marketers with a new tool for strategic management of service details' (Kingman-Brundage, 1989: 30), enabling management to make decisions on service system design, marketing, quality control, human resource and technological management. Complexities are simplified, clarifying service functions and their interrelationships in a simple and useful way to management (Chadee and Mattsson, 1996), and helping employees understand their impact on the customer's experience (Gutek *et al.*, 2000).

The contribution of the consumerist gap approach to service blueprinting is to demonstrate that if the design works against the service it is likely that clients will experience dissatisfaction because staff are less likely to deliver the performance standards expected of them. The method provides ways to investigate specific situations by examining the clients' perspectives, free of the underlying technological, regulatory and commercial realities, although these of course provide the contexts to managerial decisions for service design.

CHAPTER 5

Service quality and tourist satisfaction

Introduction

On several occasions so far the terms 'quality', 'service quality' and 'customer satisfaction' have been used, but without formal definition. This chapter explores the meanings of these terms and brings together a number of key issues which need to be clarified before further analysis of tourism and hospitality service design and delivery systems can be developed. This chapter also reviews the influential SERVQUAL method and model.

Definitions of quality

In the manufacturing sector the concept of quality is widely accepted. The basis is technical specifications for components, dimensions and performance. The statistical measurement of a run of products for divergence from specifications such as advocated by Shewart (1931) laid a foundation for the evaluation of the costs of defects as an answer to the question 'how much quality is enough?' Feigenbaum (1956) developed the notion of total quality control starting with the design of the product and ending only when the product has been placed in the hands of a customer who remains satisfied. He also stressed the need to recognize that quality is everyone's job, thus initiating the strategic approach to quality management advocated in this book.

Garvin (1988: 27) has remarked that 'despite the interest of managers, quality remains a term that is easily misunderstood . . . Scholars in four disciplines – philosophy, economics, marketing and operations management have . . . each viewed it from a different vantage point.' Thus, even in the case of manufactured goods, the management of quality is problematic. Part of the problem arises from the differing views of its meaning and significance taken between the various functions of one company as a consequence of their task cultures and traditions. 'But all share a common problem, each is vague and imprecise when it comes to describing the basic elements of product quality' (ibid.: 31). His concern led him to make a comprehensive study of quality in products and services, from which he was able to classify quality in five ways.

Transcendent quality varies between individuals and over time, and can be understood in the common phrase 'I know it when I see it'. An approach relying on the measurable features of the product, an *expert view of quality*, leads to design specification and technical drawings. *User-based quality*, while in part based on individual judgement, is also the basis of consumer legislation which introduced the test of merchantability, requiring goods sold commercially to be fit for their purpose: the classic test was that a bucket should not leak. *Manufacturing quality* is concerned to minimize deviations from the standards set in technical specifications. Goods meeting internal specifications therefore conform to the manufacturer's requirements, whether or not customers are satisfied. The fifth classification is *value-based quality*.

Issues in service quality

Harington and Akehurst (1996) undertook a detailed review of 21 leading articles on the topic of service quality, and from this they identified some 60 terms used by various authors to define the dimensions of quality. Examination of their data indicates that the most frequently discussed general factors were service delivery and interactions (14), standards of performance (12), technical factors (10) and image (7). In the terminology of Scandinavian writers, particularly Grönroos, the two fundamental aspects to quality are the technical quality provided by the company and the functional quality: how it is perceived by the client. Elaborating on this, he wrote:

> what customers receive in their interactions with the firm is clearly important to them and to their quality evaluation. Internally this is very often thought of as the quality of the product delivered. However, this is not the whole truth. It is merely one quality dimension, called the technical quality of the outcome of the service production process . . . However, as there are a number of interactions between the provider and the customer,

including more or less successfully handled moments of truth, the technical quality dimension will not count for the total quality which the customer perceives has already been received. The customer will obviously also be influenced by the way in which the technical quality, the outcome or end result of the process is transferred to him or her . . . This is the functional quality of the process. (Grönroos, 1990: 57)

It is interesting to note Grönroos's recent reappraisal of the perceived service quality concept. He emphasizes that service firms have no product, only interactive processes built from resources, and a governing system. The resources are employees, physical assets, technology and systems, and the firm's customers. The process through which services are created is interactive marketing, internal to the firm, and supported by traditional external marketing activities through which clients are attracted. The consumer perceives what he or she receives as the outcome of the technical processes.

But he or she also, and often more importantly, perceives how the process itself functions . . . Originally I never thought that the perceived service quality model would be anything more than a conceptual model that would help researchers and practitioners to understand the needs satisfying elements of a market model in a service context . . . in retrospect, I should probably have used the terms 'technical and functional features of services' instead of 'technical and functional quality dimensions of services'. We should probably have had a model of perceived service features instead of perceived service quality. (Grönroos, 2001: 151–2)

The degree of quality experienced in a service transaction can be considered to give rise to a level of satisfaction which may vary between customers. Lewis and Booms (1983) identified the following factors as significant in understanding this variability in the enjoyment of services:

- Service quality is more difficult for the consumer to evaluate than the quality of goods.
- Service quality perceptions result from a comparison of consumer expectations with actual service performance.

• Quality evaluations are not made solely on the outcome of a service; they also involve evaluations of the process of service delivery.

An important theme underlying the discussion in this book, and found throughout the literature on service quality, is concerned with understanding the meaning and significance of customers' perceptions of a service. Perception is the basis for personal interpretation of the world. Given the wide range of stimuli to which we are exposed, it has been argued that

> people tend to select from the myriad stimuli to which they are exposed those which appear to be relevant to their needs. Information, for example, will be filtered through the mesh of personal interests, attitudes, motivational structure, social background, and cultural influences. Existing personal cognitive structures will also affect . . . the individual. (Chisnall, 1985: 98)

By extension, perception is also important in the judgement consumers make of the quality of a product or service. Wilkie (1986:551) argues that two key factors determine how something is perceived: its stimulus characteristics and the characteristics of the consumer. He continues by indicating that 'The issue of which stimuli consumers choose to perceive becomes a key question.' The question of individually perceived service standards underlines the problem for managers seeking to design and deliver services satisfying the expectations of many clients. Others have discussed the significance of the point, and the difficulties which result.

> Customer perceived quality is rather a blend of objective facts and subjective judgements, of knowledge as well as ignorance. . . . Nor can manufacturers consider themselves experts . . . Quality has become an integrating concept between production orientation and marketing orientation. (Gummesson, 1988: 9)

Szybillo and Jacoby (1974) have distinguished between internal cues – the specific characteristics of the product – and external cues including the price, brand images and promotional messages employed in its marketing. 'Either singly or in composite, such cues provide the basis for perceptions concerning product quality' (ibid.: 76).

Moving even further from the 'hard' and measurable concerns of much of the literature dealing with the management of quality, Campbell (1987) argued that day dreaming and anticipation are central to the process of consumption in modern society. In this view, satisfaction is not derived so much from the purchase and use or consumption of products, as from anticipation of pleasure. The fundamental motivation for consumption (once essential needs are met) is to experience pleasure, but since reality is imperfect, any purchase might result in disillusionment. The significance of this for the consumerist gap study can be understood from arguments such as Urry's that most tourism purchases present a particular characteristic which make them prone to result in dissatisfaction for the client. He concludes that they are

> constructed in our imagination through advertising and the media, and through the conscious competition between different social groups . . . Tourism daydreams are not autonomous, they involve working over advertising and other media generated sets of signs. Almost all the services provided to tourists have to be delivered at the time and place at which they are produced. As a consequence, the quality of the social interaction between the provider of the service, such as the waiter, flight attendant or hotel receptionist, and the consumers, is part of the product being purchased by tourists. If aspects of the social interaction are unsatisfactory . . . then what is purchased is in effect a different service. The problem results from the fact that the production of such consumer services cannot be entirely carried out backstage, away from the gaze of the tourist. (Urry, 1990: 77)

More pragmatically, Zeithmal, Berry and Parasuraman (1988) argue that the customer reaches a judgement about the quality of service actually experienced when measured against the perceived service (based on the determinants of satisfaction discussed above). Similarly, the consumerist gap model provides a way of investigating the quality of service experiences from the perspective of the client.

Table 5.1 summarizes a study by Albrecht and Zemke (1985) of the factors which airline passengers consider to be most important in their flying experience. Commenting on this study, Grönroos (1990) pointed out that spontaneity and recovery were new issues at that time, and are functional aspects of quality, but only problem solving is a technical aspect of service management. This distinction is congruent with the service delivery/service design nexus which this book seeks to investigate. Some of the case studies distinguish between effective and inappropriate responses to passengers' needs following technical failures, and analysis often demonstrates that it is the soft, interactive aspects of the way these incidents are handled which determines customers' ultimate satisfaction. The consumerist gap acid test is not that a delayed flight eventually arrives at its destination; managers must also be concerned with how their passengers feel about the airline on arrival.

Table 5.1 *Passenger perceptions of airline service quality*

Factor	Example	Outcome
Care and concern	Assisting an aged passenger through the airport	A feeling that the organization, its staff and its operational system are devoted to solving their problems
Spontaneity	Steward notices a passenger is unhappy about something and offers assistance	A willingness and readiness to approach customers and take care of their problems
Problem solving	Passenger who misses a flight is offered a different routing	Contact employees are skilled in their duties and perform according to standards, and are supported by the organization's systems
Recovery	Passenger who checks in late is fast-tracked through the airport and on to the plane by a member of the check-in staff	Trust that if anything goes wrong or something unexpected happens there is someone who is prepared to make a special effort to handle the situation

Based on Albrecht and Zemke (1985)

Gaps between expectations and service experiences

The study of consumer satisfaction is often based on identifying and understanding the gaps which may be perceived by customers between what they had anticipated and their experiences of the service. Various approaches exist to conceptualize expectations. Clow *et al.* (1997) suggest that the predicted level of service is based on what the firm promises in its advertising, word of mouth, and past experiences. In expectancy theory customers predict what they expect to be the outcome of a service (Tolman, 1932). The consumerist gap model argues that the expectations which a customer has prior to a service influence their evaluation of the firm's performance, and affect their satisfaction. Another approach regards expectations as the level of performance the customer wants from the firm, and is the basis for the SERVQUAL instrument discussed below.

· In the consumerist gap model (see Figure 4.5 on page 74), customers' expectations of service standards are indicated by the level A_0 on the continuum from dissatisfaction to satisfaction. The model leaves unquantified the exact nature and level of satisfaction anticipated. This has the advantage of allowing it to fluctuate both between passengers on one flight and between the various flights undertaken by individual passengers. The model therefore accepts expectations as a fuzzy concept, rooted in individual experiences, moods and values, and it views experiences evaluated by individuals in terms of their perceptions of complex factors in the delivery of services, including notably the technical (Type A) and interactive (Type B) elements discussed throughout this book. The expectations paradigm has both supporters and challengers. Some of the main issues are discussed in Clow *et al.* (1997) and in Hill and Alexander (2000). Chenet, Tynan and Money (1999) provide an interesting discussion of issues which arise when differences occur between the specification of a service (that is to say, its managers' expectations) and service performance.

SERVQUAL

The SERVQUAL model is concerned with a spectrum of linked service gaps impinging on service quality. The general SERVQUAL model combines perceptions of service quality on five dimensions: *tangibles, reliability, responsiveness, assurance* and *empathy* (Parasuraman, Zeithmal and Berry, 1988). These were reduced from ten items in the earliest version: 'assurance' now encompasses the dimensions of *competence, courtesy, credibility* and *security*; while 'empathy' includes *access, communications* and *understanding the customer*. The three authors developed a method to identify positive and negative gaps in the firm's performance on the five service quality dimensions (Table 5.2). This was achieved using two sets of 20 statements which compare customers' expectations with their perceptions of the firm's service performance, each rated on a seven-point Likert scale. Zeithmal, Parasuraman and Berry (1990: 24–5) explain their method in the following terms:

> we followed well established procedures for devising scales to measure constructs that are not directly observable. We developed 97 items capturing the ten dimensions of service quality identified in our exploratory phase. We then recast each item into a pair of statements – one to measure expectations about firms in general within the service category being investigated, and the other to measure perceptions about the particular firm whose service quality was being assessed . . . A seven point scale accompanied each statement . . . We refined and condensed the 97 item instrument . . . to eliminate items that failed to discriminate well . . . the final instrument consisted of 22 items, spanning the five dimensions of service quality . . . tangibles, reliability, responsiveness, assurance and empathy.

Table 5.2 *General service gaps*

---

(1) Differences between consumer expectations and management perceptions of consumer expectations
(2) Differences between management perceptions of consumer expectations and service quality specifications
(3) Differences between service quality specifications and the service actually delivered
(4) Differences between service delivery and what is communicated about the service to consumers
(5) Differences between consumer expectations and perceptions of the quality of the service received; depending on the size and direction of the other four gaps

---

Based on Parasuraman, Zeithmal and Berry (1985)

Discussing their findings from a comparative study of four service industries – banking, long distance telephone, repair and maintenance, and credit cards – the research team Zeithmal, Parasuraman and Berry showed that reliability was regarded as the most critical dimension of service quality to their research samples in each service sector studied. 'Reliability' in this context means the ability to perform the promised service dependably and accurately.

SERVQUAL and tourism

Parasuraman, Zeithmal and Berry have pointed out in several of their publications that the other factors may be more significant as cues influencing potential customers. This point should be considered in the context of the varying degrees of consumer involvement with services. The factor which mattered least to current customers was *tangibles* (the appearance of physical facilities, equipment, personnel, and communications materials). In my view, there is evidence which directly refutes this. Tangibles have been shown in many studies to be significant in tourism, both in consumer choice and in their service experiences. A senior airline manager once remarked to me that when confronted with a broken reading light over his seat, one passenger had loudly demanded to see the aircraft's maintenance log, fearing that the engines might be in the same condition!

In Figure 5.1 it can be seen that each of the five gaps can potentially cause dissatisfaction with a holiday. Gap 1 is the result of any mismatch between what customers expect and managers' perceptions of what customers want from their holiday. Even if gap 1 does not cause problems, further difficulties might cause dissatisfaction. Gap 2 relates to problems in the technical specifications for a holiday, for example the tour operator might schedule a 6 a.m. departure to optimize use of an aircraft. However, this departure time could necessitate an extra night's hotel accommodation and additional expense for those passengers unable to reach the airport from home at that hour. Gap 3 describes the varied set of circumstances which sometimes occur, such as travel delays. Gap 4 can arise from exaggerated advertising claims. Any or all of these four gaps contribute to gap 5, which is comparable to the consumerist gap acid test discussed earlier in which the customer compares his or her own experiences with what was expected from the service.

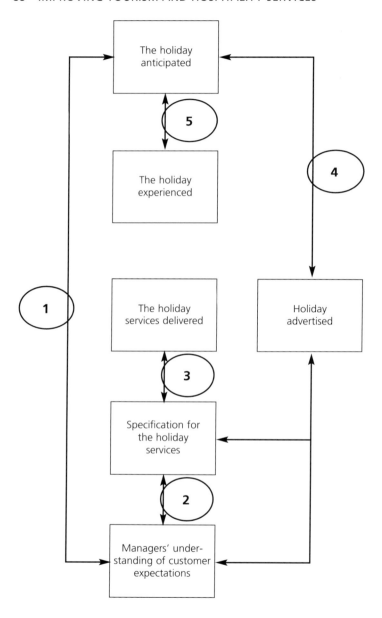

Figure 5.1 *SERVQUAL: a tourism application*

The SERVQUAL debate

SERVQUAL has been criticized both for its underlying concept-ualization and its methodology (Carman, 1990; Brown, Churchill and Peter, 1993; Teas, 1994; Buttle, 1995; Johns, 1999). Some researchers even question the continuing use of SERVQUAL:

> At best, it can be argued that SERVQUAL is applicable to contexts close to its original setting, that is, appliance repair, retail banking, long distance telephone . . . it is questionable . . . whether it is measuring service quality at all. (Robinson, 1999: 29)

Nevertheless, it has been applied to various sectors of tourism and hospitality in a number of studies, for example Fick and Ritchie (1991); Saleh and Ryan (1992); Stevens, Knutson and Patton (1995); Tribe and Snaith (1998); Mok and Armstrong (1996); Tan and Pawitra (2001); Robledo (2001).

Debate still continues on the appropriateness of the gap approach, including its core constructs of consumer satisfaction, expectations and quality (Chadee and Mattsson, 1996). Bitner, Booms and Tetreault (1990) have suggested that perceived service quality, in contrast to the quality of individual service transactions, may be similar to an individual's general attitude towards the service firm, a point of view which echoes Grönroos's three factor model discussed in Chapter 2.

Many contemporary researchers investigating the related issues of service quality and the ways in which customers experience service episodes continue to refer their work to the SERVQUAL model, either by directly employing some or all of its constructs, or by explicitly attempting to differentiate their analysis from what has become the benchmark of modern service management research. Although it has been subjected to severe criticism, SERVQUAL (developed and refined by Zeithmal, Berry and Parasuraman in a series of articles and books spanning more than a decade and a half), continues to serve us well in two important respects: it highlights unequivocally the centrality of quality in service research and man-agement, and it emphasizes the complexity of managing service experiences.

Dissatisfaction with services

The opposite of service quality is service failure, the consequence of which is customer dissatisfaction. Dissatisfaction has been defined as a state of cognitive or affective discomfort. The consumer has allocated some of his or her resources, spending money and time, and building up an anticipation of satisfaction. But if the customer's judgement of the service when experienced is that it did not meet expectations, he or she will experience cognitive dissonance (Festinger, 1957). The response to any dissonant experience is an effort to correct the situation, or a determination to avoid it in the future. Nevertheless, passengers often have to travel with airlines which had previously provided a dissatisfying flight, either because they were already ticketed for a further journey, or because of factors such as the convenience of that airline's schedules, its pricing, or because their itineraries are booked by their employers or a tour operator.

Dissatisfaction with the products of any organization has consequences for the organization and the customer (Boulding *et al.*, 1993). From the company's point of view, dissatisfaction represents a potential loss of the customer's future business as he or she can easily migrate to an alternative provider in the hope of experiencing better outcomes (Ahmad, 2002). An extension of this argument is that the disappointed customer will tell his or her friends, relatives and colleagues about the poor experience, and so may also cause that company a loss of potential business (Anderson, Fornell and Lehmann, 1994). Furthermore, dissatisfied customers often complain, causing extra work for staff as they try to placate an irate consumer (Harari, 1999; Varca, 1999; Sparks, 2002). This can be emotionally draining and time consuming, and often occurs in situations where other customers require speedy attention to their routine needs. If the complainant is still dissatisfied, formal complaints require the attention of managers and may escalate to legal procedures tying up yet more of the company's resources.

The consumerist gap research suggests that competent technical responses to any problem, such as moving the passenger who expresses discomfort to a preferred seat, are judged by the client in terms of the perceived attitude of staff. His or her satisfaction will be boosted more by what he perceives to be a caring response to a fault in the service than by someone who is merely competent in rectifying the presenting problem. Grudging service when remedying a defect, even when efficient in 'hard' performance measures, may prejudice a future purchase of that company's services (Levesque and McDougall, 2000).

The significance of the contact staff's attitudes becomes more important when the technical response to a problem proves inadequate; and in the bounded conditions of an aircraft in flight this has often been observed to be the case as was shown in Case study 3.1 (meal service). However, when staff are concerned to help the passenger, and are seen trying to overcome the particular difficulty he or she encountered, they can minimize overall dissatisfaction, thus keeping open the possibility of a future sale. In summary, the responses to an initial problem can accentuate or attenuate the dissatisfaction caused by a service interruption (of whatever nature).

The costs of managing service quality

Several studies have demonstrated a consistent positive link between quality and a firm's bottom line performance (Rapert and Wren, 1998; Fojt, 1996). Organizations incur costs from any service failure, but implementing a quality control system to minimize problems also imposes costs (Lockyer and Oakland, 1981; Bitner, Booms and Tetreault, 1990; Leppard and Molyneux, 1994; Bejou and Palmer, 1998). These costs result from actions taken to get a service right from the start, auditing that it is correctly delivered, and the expenses of responding to any failure. Further costs are incurred in implementing preventative measures to reduce future dissatisfaction, including the redesign of service delivery systems or training and motivational programmes for staff.

These costs have to be considered against the probability that dissatisfied customers will take their future business elsewhere (Hauser and Clausing, 1988; Heskett et al., 1994; Schmenner, 1995; Anderson, 1998; Zeithmal, 2000; Pyo, 2002). It has also been demonstrated that unhappy customers are likely to discuss their negative experiences with many friends and colleagues, thereby further undermining the company's marketplace credibility.

A concise summary of the argument so far is that, while tourist satisfaction is complex, it can be managed effectively. Case study 5.1 illustrates many of the points discussed above in the context of one of Britain's major historic tourist attractions.

CASE STUDY 5.1

Managing visits to castles

Historic buildings such as castles are familiar sights throughout Europe, presenting an imposing, solid appearance with their high walls and fortifications, whose original purpose was usually to keep unwanted visitors out. This is part of their attraction to contemporary visitors, but the structure of their interiors, with narrow, uneven and dark staircases and complex corridors, also presents difficulties to tourists trying to negotiate them. Typically, tourists' experience of visiting most castles is now highly organized, as a result of management decisions about how to control the flow of large numbers of people through a sequence of sights and activities determined by each castle's individual location, configuration and special features. This control is essential to minimize congestion and to ensure safety both for the artefacts on display and for visitors, since many historic buildings have winding, uneven staircases, and their many dark corridors can disorient tourists.

In most historic buildings, visitors are either accompanied by a guide, or encounter custodians located in each major exhibit area. In castles, these points of contact are important in providing visitors with information to help them enjoy their visit, but also ensure that every visitor follows the predetermined sequence through the building's internal spaces and exhibits. Tourists also come into contact with staff at catering and retail outlets, and when participating in any of the activities which form an increasing feature of visits to historic buildings and their grounds, including displays of traditional skills such as archery or falconry, or crafts, and when attending musical or other performances.

Leeds Castle

Leeds Castle is one of Britain's leading historic attractions, and is often featured prominently in English Tourist Board and other high profile international promotions. Its striking design and its location in a beautiful lake and country park provide a unique setting for many cultural and other events attracting local, national and international audiences.

The origins of the Castle have been traced to Saxon times, when a wooden manor was built for the royal family near the village of Leeds in Kent. After the Norman Conquest of England in 1066, the country was subdued by the construction of stone castles, and Robert de Crevecoeur started to build his Castle on the present site around 1119. A century and a half later, following the battles of Lewes and Evesham, his great-great-grandson was obliged to yield the Castle to Sir Roger de Leyburn, a supporter of the King. In 1287, his son conveyed Leeds Castle to 'the august prince and my most dear Lord Edward the noble King of England and my fair Lady Elinor Queen of England' (Leeds Castle Foundation, 1994: 73).

After parking their cars or leaving their coach, visitors enter the grounds through the ticketing gate with adjacent shops, refreshment and toilet facilities. Visitors can then undertake any of the activities available, in whatever sequence appeals to them, although within the Castle their tour follows a strict sequence.

The technique employed for this study was a development of the diary method used in recording service events and experiences during journeys by air. The diary records made by the researcher and an assistant were discussed between them shortly after the visit, and compiled into one agreed record. An important procedural issue is the researcher's own role as participant. It could be argued that the researcher and his assistant are not typical visitors, in that the research was their main motivation for the visit reported here. Consequently their focus of attention was the events experienced during the visit (rather than the details of the Castle).

Table 5.3 gives a brief account of each event which affected satisfaction, indicating whether it increased (+) or depressed (–) satisfaction. Overall satisfaction with the visit cannot be computed by arithmetic comparison of the number of positive and negative experiences; their significance is in assisting in the identification of actual or potential problem areas for managerial consideration.

Table 5.3 *Satisfaction diary of a visit to Leeds Castle*

Account of experience	Effect on satisfaction
1 After parking, we walk towards the entrance to the Castle grounds, but a barrier across the roadway and buildings to each side confuse us.	–
2 We queue behind a school group for tickets; after a while a steward indicates another ticket counter for individuals.	–
3 We wish to buy a film; the shop is crowded.	–
4 The group of youngsters is now blocking the main entrance, and we feel concerned that we may be in for a noisy visit.	–
5 The group waits for all members to pass the entrance, so we walk ahead quickly.	+
6 The Castle comes into view across the lawn. The sun is shining and we are again glad that we decided to visit.	+
7 As we get nearer, a dark cloud obscures the sun. We begin to wonder if we should go back to the car for our coats, but decide not to.	–
8 The stonemason's plaque in the Barbican catches our attention, and we look more closely at the old walls.	+
9 I want to take a photo of the Castle framed by the archway, but have to wait while a long stream of people walk through it.	–
10 As we walk towards the Castle, two stewards jovially direct us away from what seems to be the main entrance.	–

Table 5.3 *continued*

Account of experience	Effect on satisfaction
11 At first we feel disappointed, but rounding the corner we see to our delight the Gloriette rising from the lake. I cannot get far enough back to photograph it, having only brought a fixed focal length lens.	+
12 A number of people have congregated around a small doorway, wondering if that is the right way in to the Castle.	–
13 We all enter and would like to know more about the cellars and barrels, and why an old stairway was walled off.	–
14 Everyone is delighted with the Heraldry room. A couple are talking animatedly to one of the staff, asking about the Field of the Cloth of Gold. Another couple are asking about the hangings to be seen in the Queen's bedroom.	+
15 There are few visitors here, and we walk through the corridors and the first exhibits at our own pace.	+
16 We catch up with a party of about a dozen people including some young children. They are noisy and move very slowly.	–
17 We enjoy viewing the living accommodation, but can't ask questions as the guide is occupied in talking in detail to other visitors.	–
18 After leaving the Castle, we stroll to the restaurant and shops. There is a school group in the courtyard and the area is quite noisy.	–
19 We are pleased with the visit, but concerned that London is not signposted at the first roundabout after we leave.	–

Conceptualizing visitor satisfaction management at Leeds Castle

The combined visit diaries, enhanced by previous knowledge of the Castle as noted above, provided the background to a semi-structured interview lasting about an hour and a half with the Managing Director of Leeds Castle Enterprises Ltd. The objective was to validate each item in the visit diaries as being one which other visitors had remarked on as a factor influencing visit satisfaction. The Managing Director was asked to give rationales for each item (these are summarized in Table 5.4). Following this interview, the notes taken were content analysed, and using simple dendograms, the 19 separate points identified in the satisfaction diaries were condensed into key factors in the service design (Ramaswamy, 1996). This indicated four key areas for management decisions: the visitor's approach to the Castle, signing, interpretation of the Castle, and flow of visitors through the Castle.

Table 5.4 *Visitor satisfaction management at Leeds Castle*

---

(1) The visitor's approach to the castle
(Points *2, 4, 6, 7* and *11* in the visit diary, Table 5.3)
The Castle was opened to paying visitors in 1974, when Leeds Castle Foundation was established. At the outset, it was decided that views of the Castle and its lake, set in spacious lawns, were to be sacrosanct. From this, it followed that the car parks and most visitor amenities were located a considerable distance from the Castle. A notice is printed on entrance tickets, and the walk is well signposted; special transport is provided in the grounds for the elderly or disabled. A duckery and attractive gardens were constructed to soften and enliven the walk, with strategically located benches. However, the use of wheelchairs inside the Castle itself is limited to three at any one time because of the many narrow staircases.

(2) Signing
(Points *1, 2, 10, 12* and *19* in the visit diary, Table 5.3)
Signs in the grounds are kept to a minimum and are presented in a consistent style, using red or grey lettering on a cream background. However, as people often fail to read the information

Table 5.4 *continued*

provided, there is a need for staff to be available to talk to visitors. At Leeds Castle, the ideal is for visitors to see a member of staff at every turning point. All staff are encouraged to interact with visitors, but for some gardeners this may be less easy. They are primarily employed for their trade skills, although some enjoy talking about their job with visitors who are often very interested in the carefully designed and tended gardens, which are also home to the national collections of catmint and bergamot.

(3) **Interpretation of the Castle**
(Points *8*, *13*, *14* and *17* in the visit diary, Table 5.3)
There is very little signage within the Castle, as it is a policy that signs would intrude on the visitors' enjoyment of the building and its contents, giving visitors more the impression of a museum than a lived-in house. During normal visiting hours, staff are stationed in each main room or area of the Castle and are expected to be proactive, responding to visitors' interests rather than reciting factual information by rote. This system enables people to move through the various parts of the Castle at a pace dictated by their own interests; some spend more time in the displays of the Heraldry room, others are more attracted by other elements such as the furnishings of the drawing room or the Thorpe Hall room. The Castle is regularly opened early for pre-booked coach parties and for special interest groups, and in these cases visitors are guided through the Castle by staff using their more specialized knowledge, and if required, in a foreign language.

The Leeds Castle guide book is now available in nine languages, as 50% of visitors are from overseas. One in seven visitors purchase a copy on entry at the ticket boxes. The large print run means that it is profitable at £2.50 per copy, although £250,000 is tied up in three years' stock. The guide book is particularly useful when visiting the grounds where there are fewer staff, but also helps expand visitor enjoyment and understanding within the Castle.

(4) **Flow of visitors through the Castle**
(Points *2*, *9*, *10*, *11*, *15* and *16* in the visit diary, Table 5.3)
The structure of old buildings such as Leeds Castle is not ideal for large numbers of visitors, and it was essential that they all

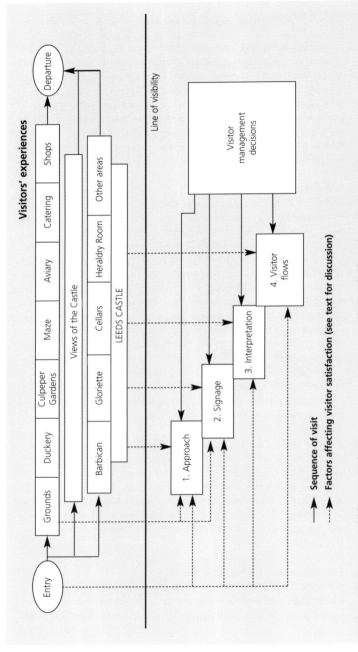

Visitors' experiences

| Entry | Grounds | Duckery | Culpeper Gardens | Maze | Aviary | Catering | Shops | Departure |

Views of the Castle

| Barbican | Gloriette | Cellars | Heraldry Room | Other areas |

LEEDS CASTLE

Line of visibility

Visitor management decisions

1. Approach
2. Signage
3. Interpretation
4. Visitor flows

→ **Sequence of visit**

⇢ **Factors affecting visitor satisfaction (see text for discussion)**

Figure 5.2 *Conceptual blueprint of visitor management at Leeds Castle (based on Laws, 1998)*

followed one route through the building. From the first day of opening the Castle to the public, it was decided that visitors would enter through the Norman cellars, thus gaining pleasure from the unique exterior view of the Gloriette (an ornate tower rising from a small island in the lake and connected to the main Castle by a corridor in a high stone arch). The visit then proceeds in chronological order through the Castle. Visitors have no choice but to follow the prescribed route through the Castle: unobtrusive rope barriers are placed to guide them.

Conceptual blueprint of visitor management at Leeds Castle

Figure 5.2 presents a conceptual blueprint of the visits to Leeds Castle. Following Shostack's convention, above the line of visibility it indicates the main features of the visit in sequence (entry, grounds, Barbican, Gloriette, Cellars, Heraldry room, other interior areas, Retail, Catering and departure). The blueprint is conceptual in that below the line of visibility it condenses the detailed managerial tasks into key aspects.

Based on Laws (1998)

Conclusion

The case study of Leeds Castle has shown how the quality of service provided at a well-managed castle can be analysed. Hospitality service quality and tourist satisfaction should be at the heart of the design and delivery of tourism services. Yet, it is very difficult for managers to be precise about how particular decisions regarding the technology or presentation of a service will be perceived by customers. One of the important points of consensus among researchers investigating service quality is that people experience services differently from one another. Unfortunately this adds a further degree of uncertainty to managers' work. A senior airline manager once remarked to me in exasperation, 'You know Eric, what passengers really want is a private jet that can land in the street outside their front door, taking them directly to their hotel!' This rueful comment suggests that it is an appropriate point in the book to turn attention to the marketing of tourist services because this provides much of the foundation for what customers anticipate.

CHAPTER 6

Marketing tourism and hospitality services

Introduction

Marketing is widely regarded as the core business function concerned with matching the organization's skills with market demand.

> The organization's task is to determine the needs, wants and interests of target markets and to deliver the desired satisfactions more effectively and efficiently than competitors in a way that preserves or enhances the customers' and the society's well being. (Kotler, 1998: 26)

Grönroos (2001) has drawn an important distinction between internal marketing, focused on the processes needed to produce the service, and the firm's external marketing activities. This chapter is mainly concerned with the latter.

The service marketing paradigm

The objective of this chapter is to highlight a number of aspects of service marketing which are important from the perspective of service quality management. In 1977 Bateson posed the question, 'Do we need services marketing?' His answer was affirmative, and he has recently updated his analysis (Bateson, 2002). Booms and Bitner (1981) suggested an expansion of the basic 4Ps marketing approach, adding *People*, *Process* and *Physical Evidence* to the well-known toolkit of *Product*, *Price*, *Promotion* and *Place* originally described by McCarthy (1960), and surely familiar to every student of marketing.

Normann (1991) went further and argued that the paradigm has changed: academic interest has moved on from the identification of the distinguishing characteristics of services, and now the theoretical and managerial marketing literature has come to accept that effective service sector management requires specialized approaches which are generally thought to be less relevant in the manufactured sectors. The term 'paradigm' is defined as 'a set of assumptions about the world which is shared by a community of scientists investigating the world' (Deshpande, 1983: 101). The main paradigm in theories of marketing strategy has traditionally been the managerial requirement to bring potential clients to the point where the action of purchasing a product yields satisfaction to the customer and profit to the vendor. More recently, it has been accepted that purchases are made to gain a range of benefits from use or ownership, leading to the 'market orientation' paradigm, and it is this which underlies the concern in this book to define the conditions under which clients are more (or less) likely to purchase future hospitality or tourism services from a particular business. Haywood (1997) and Laws (2002) have reviewed the relevance of the marketing concept for tourism. The issue is not confined to tourism: the wider context to this situation is the growth of consumer-rights awareness (Prus, 1989), and the 'metacontext' of scepticism about the underlying values and institutions of Western societies (Hughes, 1993).

The significance of influencing consumer choice

The purpose of marketing is to obtain (and retain) customers by ensuring that the service offered is attractive to target groups, and by influencing their decision to purchase. The contexts include the marketplace within which the firm operates, its own competitive capabilities, and consumers' attitudes towards it.

Consumer decision taking represents a choice between many alternative allocations of time and funds, and these choices can cause anxiety about the correctness of the decision taken.

Many researchers agree that personal sources of information, including previous experience and word of mouth recommendations from friends and acquaintances, is the most important factor in risk reduction strategies when trip planning (Raitz and Dakhil, 1989; Fodness and Murray, 1997). Dellaert, Ettema and Lindh (1998) argue that tourists' decisions are complex with multifaceted elements, which are interrelated and evolve over time. The key factors in holiday choice are varied, and can include cost, availability, or various psychic benefits such as the exclusivity or relative newness of a particular type of holiday component including specific hotels, modes of transport or available activities. Thus, tourist information search is a lengthy process involving a sequence of steps (Raaij, 1986).

This risk-based approach to modelling consumer choice (see Table 6.1) is helpful because it focuses attention on the emotive judgemental nature of many tourists' involvement with their holiday experiences. One method by which consumers can reduce the potential risk of making an unsatisfactory purchase is to seek information beforehand, by informal word of mouth from friends or from formal marketing communication sources such as advertising, brochures or sales staff.

Table 6.1 *Tourist choice and risk*

Aspect of choice	Destination issue	Role of information	Most salient sources of information
Complexity	Where?	Answers specific queries; raises other issues; compounds the difficulty of choice	Travel agent; VICs (etc.); media; advertising; Internet
Risk	Will it be: fun? safe? too costly?	Reassurance	Experience; friends; travel writers; travel agent
Choice	Would an alternative have been better?	Information streams coming from competing destinations	Friends' holiday anecdotes; travel writers
Experience	Quality and style	N/A	Destination services
Evaluation	Future bookings by this client and friends	N/A	Experience; friends' anecdotes

In any industry, business success depends on each firm's ability to identify and influence the flows of customers (and ensuing revenue). Fornell and Wernerfelt (1987) have distinguished between four flows, shown in Table 6.2. In tourism, a fifth factor is often important, particularly for retail agency staff whose reward structure is partly based on incentives from airlines and hotels (Laws, 1997; Swarbrooke, 2001). They often try to encourage customers to trade up: for example, from economy to business class, or from a standard room to a suite, or from short-haul to long-haul destinations. Similarly, a skilled waiter can often be heard to suggest to diners that they might enjoy a particular dish, or that it would be complemented by a good wine, or he might suggest a fine cognac after the meal. In each of these instances the customer is being offered enhancements to the core service, and consequently his or her expectations of the service are somewhat elevated.

Table 6.2 *Customer flows*

(1)	additional customer entry into the market
(2)	brand shifting
(3)	customer market exit
(4)	changes in purchase frequency
(5)	encouraging customers to trade up

Based on Fornell and Wernerfelt (1987); fifth flow added

Core and enhanced services

Tourism and hospitality companies can compete by making their service different from competitors through enhancements to the basic service. Marketing theorists have pointed out that all purchases are made to satisfy needs. Any item purchased must be able to perform the function claimed of it, and for which it was primarily acquired; this is the core of the product. Thus, the core of an airline's market offering is its capability to transport its clients safely from airport A to airport B at the times agreed. However, all airlines have this capability, and it seems that consumers often have in mind a more complex concept, one which includes a wider range of benefits. It has also been argued that customers buy a total package which has the combined characteristics of solving their purchasing problems. It is these additional features of products which were identified as the locus of competition: 'The new competition is not between what companies produce in their factories, but between what they add . . . in the form of packaging, services, customer advice, financing . . . and other things that people value' (Levitt, 1969: 89).

The core service is the basic market competency of the firm, but it is insufficient as the basis for commercial success in a highly competed market, one with low barriers to entry. As Rapert and Wren (1998) and Kotler and Armstrong (1999) explain, to best satisfy their customers, a producer has to offer an augmented product. In common with most other businesses, airlines offer more than basic transport in an attempt to succeed against competition, whether from other airlines or alternative modes of transport. The enhanced airline product includes physical comfort to specified standards, in-flight entertainment, and a stylish, appetizing meal or beverage service. Other improvements to the basic transport service include airport facilities and special attention to passengers' individual needs, as each airline seeks to create an image as part of its marketing strategies to distinguish its appeal from other companies. For airlines, additional features of their service may include attention to individual wishes, enhanced comfort, varied menus, in-flight entertainment, frequent-flyer schemes or improved procedures at their terminals.

Figure 6.1 shows how one company (A) might develop its core service with a few simple enhancements, while in a contrasting approach the several enhancements are carefully selected and given greater prominence than the (still essential) core service in a competing company's (B) promotions. In the case of airlines, business class offers clients more spacious accommodation, better meals and other benefits above the basic transport service, yet airlines invest heavily in differentiating their own business class from that of other airlines. Examples of enhancements to business class include limousine transfers on departure; personal video players on board; fine wines and champagne; meals served at the seat, on to china; wider seats with more leg-room and better recline angles, or seats that convert into flat beds.

Concorde represented another order of magnitude of refinements enhancing the basic transport service, not only with its unique cachet of supersonic flight, but by providing the highest possible standards of service both in the air and on the ground, with dedicated lounges at the airports served.

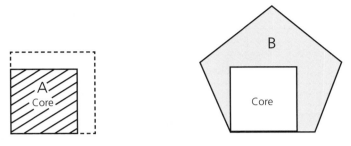

Figure 6.1 *Marketing core and enhanced services*

Given the purpose of enhancements to the core service, it is important to concentrate resources on those features which will attract customers (Wisner, 1999). A variety of formal research techniques, such as surveys, focus group work, participant observation and content analysis of unsolicited correspondence, can provide realistic and revealing insights into what is significant from the customers' perspectives (Hayes, 1998; Noe, 1999; Gilbert and Parhizgari, 2000; Hill and Alexander, 2000). Another approach is to identify aspects of the current service which consumers do not enjoy in order to improve them. Service blueprinting and consumerist gap methods can be used to generate data of this type which can help prioritize those aspects of the service requiring development or attention. A related issue is concerned with the ways in which a new competitor or an innovation by an existing competitor can attack the strength of an incumbent service provider. Rafii and Kampas (2002) have investigated six stages of disruption (see Table 6.3). In each of these, various contributing factors can each be specified for a particular business context, and then rated on a seven-point scale from enables disruption to disables disruption.

I have referred previously to the creative development of tourism service concepts, and also to the entrepreneurial style of management found in many tourism and hospitality organizations. Crawford (1997) regards both product development and innovation as a firm's responses to clear market demand. But a range of factors within the firm distinguish product development (an incremental and evolutionary process) from innovation, as indicated in Table 6.4. Edvardsson, Hagland and Mattsson (1995) argue that effective new service development depends on three factors: market synergy; the organizational context, particularly leadership and inertia or resistance to change; and market research.

Table 6.3 *Service innovation and competition*

	Hotel sector example	
Stage	Factor enabling disruption	Factor disabling disruption
Foothold market entry	Easy to establish a low service/low price hotel in the area	Lack of skill or capital to develop new hotel
Main market entry	Capital available for invest-ment	No suppliers or marketing channels for new entrant
Customer attraction	New ways of operating hotel offer benefits to customers	High standards and wide range of services
Customer switching	Variable service standards in incumbent hotel	Attractive loyalty pro-gramme for existing customers
Incumbent retaliation	Senior management of incumbent hotel resistant to change	Lack of support for new entrant from suppliers or marketing channels
Incumbent displacement	Innovation significantly dis-places incumbent's product	Volatile market sector

Service bundles

Horovitz and Panak (1992) recommend a balanced combination of different offerings to satisfy the customer, a service package combining strategic and tactical service management approaches. They define strategic service management as having three interrelated elements:

1. doing the right job, based on
2. correctly evaluating what the customer expects, and
3. creating service packages which reflect those expectations.

At a tactical level, the requirements of operational service management are about doing the job right. 'Customer expectations must not only be met in service design, but also in service delivery, ensuring

Table 6.4 *Tourism service development and service innovation*

Product development	Innovation
• Open-minded and supportive managers • Good knowledge of market • Successful existing product • Technical proficiency	• Visionary service leader • Challenging goals for new products • Good rewards • Ready access to development funding • Ability to anticipate future market demand • Good communication between technical and marketing functions • Willingness to accept failure of some projects

Based on Barclay, Holroyd and Poolton (1994); Edgett (1994); Edvardsson, Hagland and Mattsson (1995)

that the service package is provided without fault' (Horovitz and Panak, 1992: 35). Garvin (1988) emphasized the need for market research if products are to offer the dimensions of quality that are of greatest interest to consumers and if they are to target a defensible quality niche. Similarly, Band (1991), arguing that organizations should create more value for their customers in order to remain competitive, has advocated the systematic examination of all facets of a company's operation to identify their contribution (active and potential, positive and negative) to customer satisfaction.

Bateson (2002) pointed out that a service has a number of components – a bundle of benefits comprised of the physical environment for the service, the effects of service personnel and other customers. He stressed the importance of presenting customers with balanced, compatible service elements. In part, the rationale for providing premium class passengers with separate lounge facilities at airports is to ensure a consistent style of quiet and spacious accommodation throughout their journey, complemented by fine wines and food.

For example, the main components of a cruise consist of transportation, accommodation, dining, shipboard entertainment, recreational activities, domestic and foreign ports of call, and shore excursions. Teye and Leclerc (1998: 154) also note that the quality of each of the product areas and the manner in which they are delivered contribute to the guest's perception, enjoyment and satisfaction with the overall vacation experience. Consequently, a poor performance in one area may negate a high performance in other areas.

Differentiating tourism services

There is a proprietorial aspect to service management. It equates somewhat to the total perceived quality approach of Grönross's model (1982) which combines the organization's image with functional and technical performance. The vision of its service enables one organization to present its service with a special style, which clearly distinguishes it from the ways in which its competitors operate, and is conceptualized for its customers in its brand image. Three aspects have to be considered when differentiating a service in tourism, as shown in Table 6.5.

As examples of service differentiation, staying in a Sheraton hotel does not give the same experience as staying in a Hilton, and the managers of these hotels intend to provide their guests with distinctive experiences. However, staying in a second Sheraton, even in another country, is intended to provide the customer with a similar experience to his or her stay in the first Sheraton. Similarly, a flight between America and Europe on British Airways is not intended to give the same experience as a transatlantic journey on KLM, United Airlines, or Air New Zealand. In both these examples the core of the service provided to customers is very similar: staying in a good hotel is essentially about getting a good night's sleep; crossing the Atlantic is mainly about getting safely and quickly to the opposite shore. But

Table 6.5 *Differentiating tourism services*

---

(1) Service strategy, providing the company with its unique identity in comparison with the competition. The strategy should be based on market research and should be aimed at meeting the needs, expectations and motivations of target customers.
(2) The system for service delivery, containing visible and invisible components designed to provide ease of access and convenience to the customer.
(3) The people who deliver the service, and form the moments of truth.

Based on Thomas (1987)

both markets are very competitive, and the commercial success of the companies operating in them depends on attracting sufficient clients and revenue to be able to operate profitably.

Brand management is increasingly recognized as a strategic management tool rather than as an abstract concept (Lawson and Balakrishnan, 1998). Bitner, Booms and Tetreault (1990) have suggested that perceived service quality, in contrast to the quality of individual service transactions, may be similar to an individual's general attitude towards the service firm. Managers can select one of three approaches to branding consistent with either functional, symbolic or experiential concepts.

> The functional brand concept refers to the problem solving capabilities of the brand such as being reliable, efficient, practical or convenient. The symbolic brand concept is tied to the reference group or ego enhancing associations to the brand, while the experiential brand concept focuses on the cognitive stimulation or sensory gratification aspects of the brand. (Park *et al.*, 1986: 121)

Branding, imagery, positioning, market segmentation, target marketing and marketing mix are therefore mutually dependent management decisions.

Positioning tourism services

Creating these differences is referred to as 'positioning' a service. The basis of market positioning is to identify some key performance dimensions which influence customers' purchasing and consumption preferences, such as degree of luxury, or cost. These are used to calibrate a map on which competitors' services are plotted according to their perceived performance on each characteristic. Market analysts can then gain a visual impression of where the market is not well served, and adapt or position their services into the most advantageous position taking into account the strength of demand, degree of competition and the likely profitability of each possible mix of service criteria. The strategy is generally used aggressively against competitors, but it has also begun to be seen as a way of forming business partnerships for destination operators.

CASE STUDY 6.1

Positioning hotels in Port Douglas, Tropical North Queensland

This case study illustrates how two hotels cooperated with destination managers in a repositioning exercise to their mutual benefit. In typical destinations these decisions are taken independently by the managers of different organizations based on their own operating criteria. It is important to note, however, that these organizations share benefits from the attributes of the place being marketed, the expectations raised in potential clients by marketing activities, and the experiences of visitors attracted to the place. Research to establish brand strategies for destinations is therefore iterative, and open-ended. Furthermore, as the case study of Port Douglas demonstrates, it involves multiple stakeholders in the brand concept for the region.

Figure 6.2 presents a positioning model based on plotting the current relative positions of the two hotels (A and B) and the destination (X); the corners of the model are formed from the four motivational groups identified in this research. Thus, the position of a hotel indicates the relative percentages of each of the four segments in its clientele. Also shown on this diagram are the target 'potential' groups for each hotel (A1 and B1). These groups have been drawn from the regional survey and they include, for each hotel, Australian visitors staying elsewhere in Tropical North Queensland who are financially capable of affording the hotel, who are already staying in a similar standard of accommodation, who are disposed to return to the region, and who plan their accommodation in advance. Based on these criteria, the 'potential' market for Hotel A is around 18% of TNQ visitors and that for Hotel B somewhat less at 15%.

The map illustrates the problem that in the current situation both hotels occupy similar spaces somewhat away from the overall position of the region (X). Their primary appeal is based on 'self-directed' and 'image-directed' components in contrast to the region overall which appeals more broadly to a mix of motivations, in particular that for specific activities. An analysis of future target groups (A1 for Hotel A and B1 for Hotel B) indicates that to maximize their potential to draw new markets, the following positioning steps need to be taken:

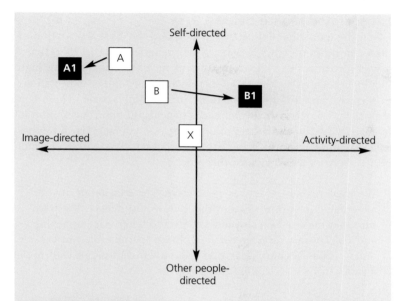

Figure 6.2 *Service positioning map*

- *To position themselves further from each other.* In the case of A this means developing imagery based more on general regional attributes while continuing to appeal to images of self-fulfilment and actualization; for B this means a greater focus on specific activities which can be conducted from the resort.

- *To position themselves closer to the region overall, as resorts within the region rather than separate from it.* While the impact upon the region overall cannot be measured by this research, it can be hypothesized that if the hotels were to pursue directions A1 and B1, this would pull the region overall closer to the midway point between the new resort positionings.

Based on Laws, Scott and Parfitt (2002)

Exaggerated service claims

Given the intangible nature of services, and the close association of their consumption with customers' self-images (Asseal, 1987), many service providers use imagery and text messages emphasizing high quality in their advertising, and thereby raise customers' expectations of service standards to a sometimes unsustainable level. There is a temptation to overstate the enhanced benefits on offer. Airlines often feature stylish, individual attention in their advertising, but it seldom feels like that, even to travellers in premium class cabins. Bennet (1991: 1) has warned against this practice:

> We used to believe it was good policy to exaggerate in our advertising, to promise more than we would deliver. We were sure that the consumer would understand what was happening and the lawyers even invented a phrase 'permissible puffery'. Today it has become clear that overblown claims can lead to disaster in the tourism business.

Two sets of issues arise: the level of service to provide, and the way it is experienced by clients. If an arbitrary decision is taken, the service provided may not match what clients anticipate. The revised standards could exceed expectations, thus increasing the company's costs unnecessarily; alternatively, too low a standard of service would offend clients, and the company would risk the loss of some of its business. The problem with service promises that are not kept is that they lead to dissatisfaction which is quite easy for consumers to articulate by pointing to the discrepancy between offer and experience. In consumerist gap terms, the anticipated service A_0 is raised to A_1 so even if the company performs well it may not reach the level that customers believe was promised to them, inevitably opening a consumerist gap which normal service delivery cannot bridge. Figure 6.3 illustrates the problem.

The difficulty is compounded when the expectation of a particular type and standard of holiday service is created by promises about a destination. Laws and Cooper (1998: 343) noted that

> resorts are comprised of a constantly shifting mosaic of stakeholders and value systems. Each of these groups has a different view of the role and future of tourism at the resort and therefore the adoption of strategies becomes a political process of conflict resolution and consensus.

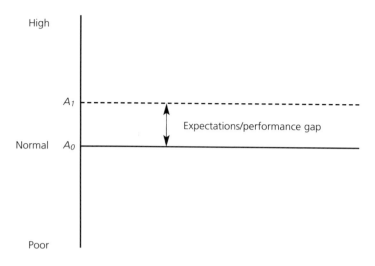

Figure 6.3 *Effects on satisfaction of exaggerated advertising claims*

A key difficulty is that the standards promised or implied in advert-
isements may not be matched by the reality of visitors' experiences
during their stay. This is significant because clients cannot sample the
destination before committing themselves to a visit, and because the
fragmented nature of the tourism industry means that many organizations are involved in delivering services to tourists during their stay,
with the potential for lack of coherent service standards. Dissatisfied
customers are unlikely to repeat their visit, and furthermore, they
tend to share their unpleasant memories on returning home.

Argenti (1997) has reviewed the literature on stakeholder theory
in management and has identified five categories of stakeholders:
investors; employees; customers; suppliers; and the relevant community. The quality of a tourism system's operations can be assessed
by examining the outcomes for each stakeholder group (Ryan, 1995).
Table 6.6 presents a summary of responses to various problems and
assesses the impacts for selected stakeholders in Canterbury's tourism
system.

Table 6.6 *Impacts for Canterbury's stakeholders*

Stakeholders	Indicative tourism problems	Responses	Observed impacts
Residents	Congestion	Attract tourists into less visited areas	Group visit pressure dispersed on to four alternative pedestrian routes. Decrease in complaints from residents living on original route. Initial complaints from residents living on new routes have now decreased.
Tourists	Congestion Limited range of attractions	New walks Signing Maps Pedestrianiza-tion New attrac-tions	Increased tourist pressure in High Street as Cathedral management measures imposed. Tourists attract peddlers and buskers – complaints from shopkeepers. Maps and signing effective in dispersing tourists.
Coach operators	Restricted and undeveloped parking	New coach park Visitor Shepherds	Complaints about length of walk to town centre and price of parking from some operators. Behaviour of tourists and congestion in town is modified by Visitor Shepherds welcoming tourists.
Cathedral	Crowds detract from experiences of visitors and worshippers	Shepherding scheme Entrance charges Burning incense	Ambience of Cathedral much improved. Visitor pressure is deflected into the town centre.

Table 6.6 *continued*

Stakeholders	Indicative tourism problems	Responses	Observed impacts
Environment	Air pollution Litter Inappropriate changes to historic buildings Wear and tear	Air quality monitoring at selected sites Park and ride to reduce cars in city New location for coach park Special planning controls	Air quality in town centre improves with increased pedestrianization. Increased air pollution at new coach park. Drivers asked not to run engines while passengers are away from coach. Special planning controls effective in maintaining historic ambience. Sheer volume of tourists overspills and widens paths provided.

Based on Laws and LePelley (2000)

Issues in pricing tourism services

The approaches which an organization adopts to pricing its services should be evaluated in the context of its overall aims, as McCarthy and Perreault (1988: 143) have pointed out:

> Managers develop a set of pricing objectives and policies in the context of the company's objectives. The policy explains how flexible prices are to be, the level at which they will be set over the life cycle of the service, and to whom and when discounts will be allowed.

Medlik (1993: 116–17), noting that price competition features strongly in the travel industry, defined this as a

> Market situation in which firms compete on price rather than quality of product or other factors to influence the buyers' choice . . . Price competition is sometimes chosen as a deliberate strategy but often is the result of unforeseen market conditions, in which planned capacity or sales exceed actual demand.

Lovelock (1994) has shown that both oversupply and lack of capacity compared to actual demand can raise unit costs. Further discussion of demand–supply imbalance and price tactics is given in Shemwell and Cronin (1994) and Tung, Capella and Tat (1997). In tactical terms, the typical response of service companies to unsold capacity is to discount it very heavily.

The result of low prices has not only been to stimulate demand for holidays currently on offer; there is also evidence of effects with long-term significance for the industry. Low prices have altered the timing of demand, for example by extending the holiday season, and have changed the demographic profile of holidaymakers, to include all age groups and most socio-economic sectors of society. Low prices have also been the locus of power plays between competing companies and between the various organizations in the holiday industry system. Several major companies including tour operators and charter airlines have failed, and there have been many take-overs and mergers between tour operators, travel retailers and charter airlines. Not all of these events can be ascribed to the results of pricing policy, but by putting the customers' focus at the point of holiday purchase on price comparisons rather than alternative destination benefits, these effects have contributed to the commoditization of holiday destinations noted and criticized by many analysts of the industry, notably Krippendorf (1987), Urry (1990) and McCannel (1992).

Pricing inclusive holidays

The complexity for a tour operator of pricing packaged holidays has been highlighted by Holloway and Robinson (1995). Robinson was the Group Marketing Manager of First Choice, one of Britain's leading tour operators, and the authors noted that the company 'produced some 2,300 brochure pages for the summer 1995 season. Most featured a price panel with perhaps 100 separate prices, making a total of almost a quarter of a million prices' (ibid.: 100). First Choice's pricing was based on a straightforward cost-plus approach, but it also reflected a range of objectives for different products, such as to regain market share in specific resorts. Further adjustments are made to achieve an overall price advantage:

> the brochure price is determined, but so too is the proposed policy on early booking discounts, child discounts, late sales reductions, travel agent commission incentives and the like. This

is because the overall profitability target of the programme must be set against the actual sales price likely to be achieved. (Ibid.)

Middleton (1991) identified 11 influences on the prices of tourism products, including high price elasticity in discretionary segments, fixed capacity, high customer psychological involvement, high fixed costs, long lead times between price decisions and product sales, and short run crisis management. Duadel and Vialle (1994) distinguished between 'spoilage' – the underutilization of resources – and 'spill' – selling too cheaply early, with the result that higher yielding demand has to be denied later on. They argued in favour of yield management techniques, using price to balance the market conditions of supply and demand. The principle of price setting for optimum yield management is based on setting various thresholds to segment customers' varying ability or willingness to pay. The relevant thresholds reflect assumptions about price-related differences in buying behaviour, particularly in respect of seasonal choices, late or early booking habits, and departure airport preferences. These can be modelled by analysis of the company's historic data (Relihan, 1989).

Seasonal pricing

One of the most common ways of setting holiday price differentials is the seasonal banding typical of tour operators' brochures and familiar to all who purchase inclusive holidays, in the form of price and departure date price matrices. This is represented schematically in Figure 6.4. The peak season, when limited discounting is undertaken because many holidaymakers are willing to pay premium prices, is shown as the broad central column, flanked by two shoulders of unequal width representing the early and late seasons. The more restricted nature of demand during the shoulder seasons limits opportunities to charge premium prices, but offers scope to stimulate market demand through a variety of discounting practices. In contrast to the generalized three-season price banding model represented in Figure 6.4 it should be noted that tour operators' brochures typically band their holidays into up to a dozen seasonal prices, although there appears to be a trend for brochures to give a base price prominently, but refer potential purchasers to complex footnotes and tables detailing a wide range of additional costs. In 2001, some British tour operators broke a long tradition by charging separately for transfers from the arrival airport to the hotel, in effect increasing the price of the advertised holiday. Not surprisingly there has been criticism of this practice among consumer groups, and adverse comments in the travel trade press.

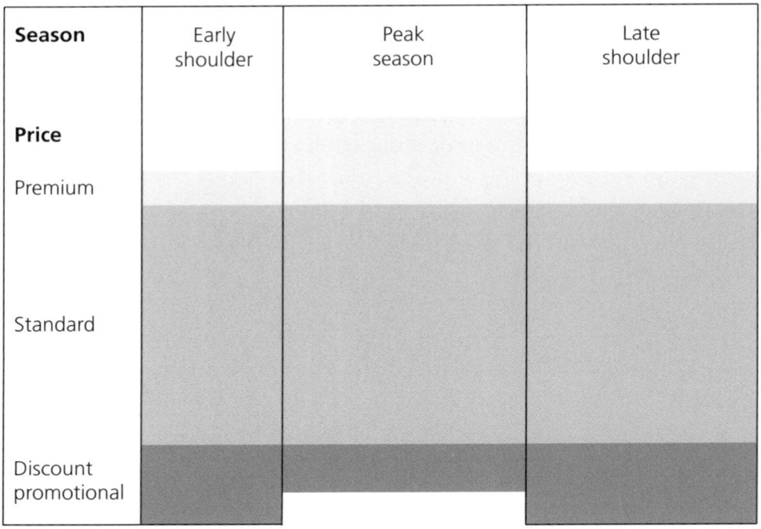

Season	Early shoulder	Peak season	Late shoulder
Price			
Premium			
Standard			
Discount promotional			

Figure 6.4 *A general model of seasonal price banding*

Late booking

Price reductions for late booking are a widespread holiday industry response to its unsold capacity, and typically are promoted by travel agents as well as tour operators shortly before departure. This has proved an effective way to tackle one of the problems characteristic of the services sector: the inability to store inventory (Cowell, 1986). Tour operators consider it advantageous to obtain some revenue for a particular holiday which they have not been able to sell at the price offered in the brochure. In addition, they are often able to obtain additional revenue by selling their own clients extra excursions and entertainment after their arrival in the resort. One common approach is to invite clients to pay a stated price, for example £150 per week, for a stated departure and duration, but leaving hotel and even the resort to the tour operator's discretion. From the customer's perspective, this introduces a higher than normal element of uncertainty (or risk) into the holiday purchase transaction.

Responses to late offers

During the 1960s and 1970s there was a highly publicized annual rush in many European countries to buy holidays as soon as the next season's brochure was launched. Queues of people formed outside travel agencies early each new year to buy holidays for the summer ahead: early purchase gave the clients the highest probability of getting their preference for destination, hotel, duration and departure date. In contrast, a trend had emerged in the 1990s to delay the purchase of package holidays. This can be understood as representing customers learning the new rules of selling, and adapting these to their own benefit when purchasing holidays. In the case of inclusive tours, the pattern of early booking which formed the basis of buyer behaviour (and consequent price adjustment tactics to shift unsold volume as departure dates approached) has altered under the influence of reduced price offers. Vellas and Becherel (1995) have identified growing resistance among clients to buying holidays early in the belief that a high proportion of capacity will remain unsold, thereby increasing the likelihood of reduced price offers, and of being able to buy a cheap holiday even if it is not in the preferred resort.

The benefits for tour operators of obtaining increased numbers of clients through the late booking discount mechanism has to be set against the difficulties which have resulted. These include (1) customers who did not obtain the quality of holiday which they had hoped for, (2) an apparent shift away from the traditional advanced booking of holidays several months ahead of departure in favour of waiting for these late offers to be made, and (3) approaches to managing both the supply and distribution channels for holidays which have tended to favour the major tour operators and the vertically integrated holiday companies strongly (Buhalis and Laws, 2001). A travel industry manager commented critically, 'getting a package deal at a knock down price is now a national sport' (Josephides, 1994). Other criticisms focus on the way that discounting is shifting holiday destination preferences. For example, flat rate holiday discounting (a prominent feature of travel retailer tactics) favours long-haul destinations, because the technique produces a greater cash saving when compared to the typically lower priced European holiday. When combined with seasonal price banding for areas such as the Caribbean, the effect has been to redistribute the peak travel season. As one senior manager commented:

all the hard work done by the tour operator and the hotelier working together in terms of spreading demand across the season is wiped out by the stroke of a felt tip pen in a travel agent's window. (Heape, 1994: 4)

The duration of the interval between clients making a booking and taking their holiday has been important to tour operators, since it provides an opportunity for them to function as 'bankers' benefiting from interest on their clients' deposits. The industry practice is for tour operators to settle their suppliers' invoices at about the time that the client receives services from the charter airline and hotel. The number of clients and the consequent aggregate value of their deposits has enabled tour operators to place money on the overnight market (Bull, 1991). This source of income is at risk from the shift towards later bookings. It is partly in response to this threat that tour operators have recently begun to offer incentives for early booking, including free child places and three weeks for the price of two. The early sale of a holiday to a consumer also has the advantage of reducing the remaining market open to competitors.

Price relativities as a signal of product quality

Kimes (1994) has suggested that consumers seem to accept yield management in the airline sector, where they receive specific benefits if they accept certain restraints. However, she raised the question of how customers react to it in other industries, suggesting that 'a customer who pays more for a similar service and cannot perceive a difference in the service may view the situation as unfair' (ibid.: 23). Kimes developed her argument on the basis of a reference price, derived from market prices and the customer's previous experience. At a normal (or reference) price, a high standard of service and amenities will please the client, but those same standards will merely be satisfactory for clients paying premium rates. Customers enjoying normal or superior standards on a holiday for which they paid low prices will be pleased, or delighted. In contrast, customers receiving normal levels of service in return for high prices will feel at best exploited, and if standards fall further, they are likely to experience (and express) anger. Low levels of service or amenities are likely to provoke negative responses whatever the price paid for them.

Garvin (1988: 44) noted that 'it seems to be difficult to determine a generally valid link between price and quality'. Value is generally regarded as meaning the delivery of more of some desired attributes of the service than the customer expected. In the short term this may occur as the outcome of deliberately underpromising, or it may result from higher than normal performance in the service delivery system. The longer term significance is that experience of superior service raises customers' expectations for future services.

Figure 6.5 suggests that customers who receive a level of service commensurate with the price they paid are likely to be satisfied with that service. They expect a 'normal' level of service if paying a 'standard' price, but better service when paying a premium. If a customer buys a discounted holiday but receives superior service he or she is likely to be delighted, but in contrast someone buying an expensive holiday and getting poor service will probably react angrily. In Chapter 1 mention was made of the high incidence of complaints about low standards for discounted holidays. An explanation can be found in Figure 6.5 which suggests that clients who receive poor standards of service are likely to feel angry and exploited irrespective of the price they paid.

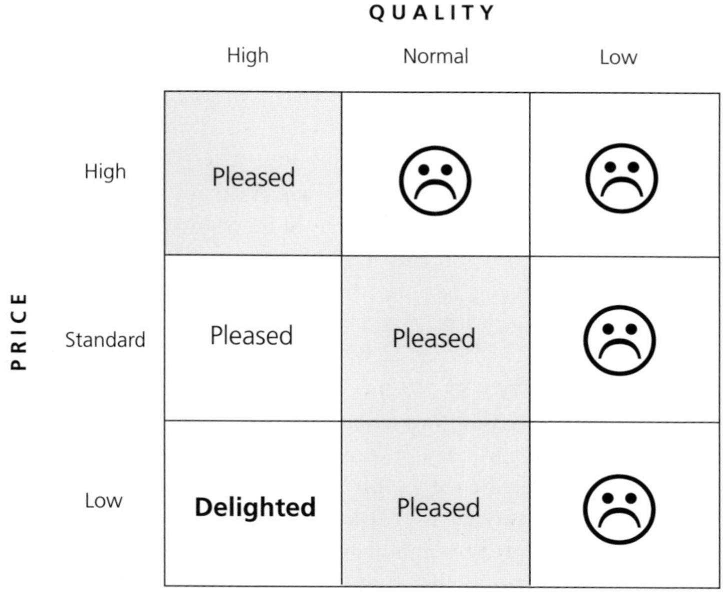

Figure 6.5 *Tourist consequences of differing price/quality combinations*

Reducing price levels and broadening market demand

A reduction in price provides increased access to the product. Ideally, the shift from one price band to a lower one occurs after the higher payers have bought, then the lower price has the effect of bringing the product to a new group of potential purchasers, with different behavioural characteristics. One example of this is the way that cruising holidays are being promoted to a broader market on the basis of reduced prices. In 1995, one tour operator new to the cruising sector claimed to have achieved its aim of gaining around 60% of cruise bookings from clients who had not cruised before. Cooney (1995: 6) reported that the Airtours Marketing Director had said,

> The [newly acquired] ship has been fully refurbished and we have made the product affordable and less formal. We have applied the Airtours sales and marketing formula, so anyone who has enjoyed our other holidays will enjoy our cruises. We have a well thought out formula. The ship is the right size to give us the economies of scale we need to offer affordable fares, which is always the starting point for customers.

Commenting on this, the Director of PSARA (Passenger Shipping Agent Retail Association) remarked that Airtours has a tightrope to walk.

> On one hand, they are telling customers there is no mystique about cruising, its just a package holiday in which the hotel floats. On the other hand, it must try not to take away the elegance of cruising because they would be selling themselves and the industry short. (Ibid.)

Customer loyalty

The assumptions underlying traditional marketing are that marketing activity has the primary purpose of attracting new customers and that the market consists of a large number of potential customers. In this simplified approach to marketing, the needs of all customers were regarded as very similar, and it was thought to be easy to replace any who desert with new customers to the extent that there was little concern with methods of retaining existing customers. In contrast, service marketing and contemporary approaches to marketing in other sectors emphasize the importance of developing long-term relationships with their customers (Berger and Nasr, 1998; Bloemer, de Ruyter and Wetzels, 1999; Edvardsson and Strandvik, 2000; Leong, Kim and Ham, 2002; Rafii and Kampas, 2002). McCarthy (1960: 288–9) commented:

> A firm can through long term relationships with customers get access to detailed and useful knowledge about the customer . . . develop a core of satisfied committed customers. . . . Service firms have started to identify their customers, which enables them to be more focused in their marketing.

Increasingly the concern expressed by tourism managers is how to understand the factors which are central in motivating clients to remain loyal to their original supplier when there are so many alternative offers of similar services and so many different services and products to enjoy, with limited funds and time.

It was demonstrated earlier, by reference to the range of satisfaction reported by a group of student travellers, that individuals confronted with any given situation experience varying degrees of satisfaction or dissatisfaction. This occurs for three reasons. Firstly, each individual approaches a service with his or her own set of expectations based on prior experience, immediate disposition and needs. An example of the second reason is the situation where a guide showing a group around a historic building could, in explaining a particular feature, excite and inform one member of the group, but bore or antagonize another. Thirdly, the combination of these two factors, varying expectations and differing experiences, can result in different levels of satisfaction for each of the customers experiencing one service.

Further consideration of tourism purchasing decisions: consumer involvement

Holidays represent a period of time when the individual is relatively free from everyday constraints, and is able to indulge his or her wishes. Holidays also represent a deliberate purchase, in which limited financial resources are invested in buying time in a chosen resort, implying both that the tourist cannot visit alternative resorts during that vacation and that he or she has chosen not to spend money and time on alternative products. Consumers' degrees of interest and 'involvement' in purchasing particular products or services range from low to high. Involvement is likely to be high when the purchase has functional and symbolic significance, and entails some financial risk (Asseal, 1987).

The purchasing decisions of customers, whether past, present or potential, are crucial to any company; existing customers generate flows of both revenue and information. The perceptions, attitudes and preferences of current clients are important data to companies seeking to understand customer behaviour. A valuable distinction has been drawn between the attitudes of customers to whom a particular purchase has personal importance, and those to whom it has merely utilitarian or routine significance (Chase, 1978). It has been suggested that customers' purchasing behaviour may be considered to be distributed along a continuum from routinized response behaviour to extensive problem solving (Howard, 1977). Customers whose involvement with tourism services is high are likely to undertake extensive search behaviour, and as the model developed in this section suggests, they are likely to be concerned with the enhanced aspects of the core product.

Consumer involvement has been defined in the following terms: 'a state of energy (arousal) that a person experiences in regard to a consumption-related activity' (Cohen (1982), cited in Wilkie, 1986). Cohen considered that involvement is high when customers are enjoying a service. He also pointed out how it occurs within specific settings. Both points are significant to the development of this study. In relation to journeys by air, the synopsis of passenger correspondence following lengthy delay (see page 15) indicates that there is a real increase in the level of arousal experienced (reported) by passengers during a service failure. Secondly, several phases have been identified in flight services, and the level of passenger involvement appears to differ between phases such as meals or events at the airport. A further factor is the significance of the distinction between core and enhanced airline services. It is suggested that passengers have varying levels of involvement in the airline service, some regarding it instrumentally as the interval between departure and arrival, others looking forward to (or dreading) the experiences en route.

Four aspects of holidays suggest that many tourists experience a high degree of involvement in choosing their holiday destination:

- Holidays are expensive
- Holidays are complex both to purchase and experience
- There is a risk that the resort may not prove satisfying
- The resort reflects the holidaymaker's personality

High involvement customers are less likely to switch to alternative suppliers, and may be more tolerant of minor service failures, in part because of a deeper understanding of the service delivery system. This theory suggests that in high involvement pre-purchase decision situations a consumer will compare brands in a detailed and systematic manner. Similarly, after purchase the consumer will evaluate the chosen brand's performance. Satisfaction will reinforce the consumer's judgement and that brand is more likely to be repurchased in the future. If dissatisfaction occurs the consumer will reassess his or her choice, and repurchase of that brand is much less likely to occur.

Low involvement decision making occurs where the consumer does not consider the product particularly important to his or her belief system and does not strongly identify with it. However, much of the argument in marketing literature, and many of the actions of marketing managers, assumes that customers are very interested in their product, when in reality they are often not. In contrast to the rational, information processing model of high involvement behaviour, the consumer who has low involvement with a particular product is likely to be a passive recipient of information about it. When a purchasing need or desire arises, one brand is likely to be purchased rather than others on the basis of some token advantage, such as ease of access, schedule convenience or familiarity; and it is widely believed that this can be gained through repetitive advertising.

The low involvement consumer will, however, be relatively neutral towards any brand as it (and the product) has no strong association with any of his or her important beliefs. Low involvement products offer solutions to consumers' problems rather than optimizing the benefits. Services are purchased on the basis of price or convenience, since the consumer has no basis for distinguishing between the benefits of various brands.

The concept of involvement is consumer related rather than product related. Asseal (1987) has suggested that the degree of consumer involvement is the critical factor in both consumer behaviour and in setting marketing strategy. Four levels of consumer involvement can be distinguished, with four distinct service outcomes for consumers. It follows that the features of a service which its managers believe distinguish it from competitors' should be defined in terms of the consumers' evaluation of the importance of each service attribute. The varying extent of consumer involvement can be measured on an individual level, and this understanding can be used as a basis for segmented approaches to a general market. Table 6.7 applies this conceptually to model satisfaction outcomes contingent upon passenger involvement of contrasting service strategies.

Low involvement passengers are satisfied if an airline provides an on-time flight with reasonable standards of comfort and catering. Any service enhancements such as a sophisticated entertainment system or fine meals are received with pleasure. In contrast, a high involvement passenger expects that enhanced service as a minimum requirement and looks for additional evidence of superior service such as the latest style of seating or enhanced facilities at the airport. The basic core service is insufficient to please a high involvement passenger.

Table 6.7 *Consumer involvement and choice between brands*

Service features	Involvement	
	High	Low
Core	sufficient	insufficient
Enhanced	grateful	expected

Based on Asseal (1987)

Time in the experience of tourist services

Market clearing is a pivotal economic concept describing how the pricing mechanism operates in unfettered marketplaces, resulting in a balance between the quantity of something which people wish to supply at a price and the quantity which others are prepared to purchase at that price. The concept that quantity purchased is likely to rise when prices are reduced is fundamental in both economic theory and marketing, although marketing practice sometimes proves the contrary case when people are demonstrated to be willing

Price

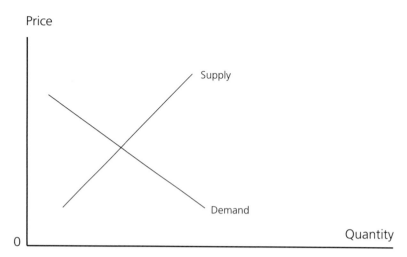

Supply

Demand

0

Quantity

Figure 6.6 *A market clearing model*

to pay premium prices, for example to travel on Concorde. Figure 6.6 illustrates the classical analysis of market clearing.

However, in the case of hospitality and tourism (and arguably for other services), there is another dimension. Since the consumption of a service such as tourism occurs over a period of time, the importance of the moment of purchase is somewhat lessened.

It seems advantageous to consider time as the third dimension to a new model (Figure 6.7), extending beyond the foreground with its familiar constructs of quantity and price/cost. This time dimension can be conceptualized as the duration of the service episode, varying from a period of hours for a journey by air to several weeks for an inclusive holiday or an extended business itinerary. During this period, the tourist experiences a wide range of interactions, any of which can affect his or her satisfaction. Here, another feature of tourism becomes critical: the industry is fragmented and many organizations are involved in customer contact and interactions, some of these are not readily influenced by the company with which the customer contracted for his or her holiday. It is the quality of the various events that the customer experiences in this time which constitute the quality of the tourism service, and this becomes a factor in any subsequent purchasing decision. In other words, the delivery of the service is the third dimension now added to the

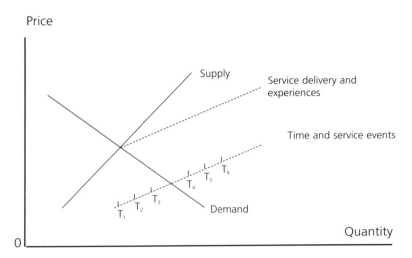

Figure 6.7 *Service consumption model*

market clearing model. During the service episode the quality of the organization's design and delivery is subjected to the consumerist gap acid test of satisfaction, with implications for repurchase and the success of a particular tourism company. In effect, the third dimension of the service consumption model (the timeline) incorporates the consumerist gap arguments presented in this book. The analysis of marketplace dynamics is no longer limited to matching supply and demand conditions, but is critically concerned with the experience of consuming the service.

The importance of service delivery is implicitly recognized in modern marketing through its orientation towards understanding the preferences of selected groups of consumers, by careful positioning of the service attributes to appeal to customers and by the specialized techniques used to promote services to them. The resources and skills of the company are then applied to meet their customers' requirements effectively and profitably. Marketing orientation is therefore the key to implementing the manager's understanding of how individuals who are potential clients of an organization make decisions to spend their resources of time, money and effort, and of the benefits they seek from so doing. Another relaxation of traditional economic theory is that it is no longer accepted that consumers make choices having gathered and evaluated all the available information about relative costs and the comparative characteristics of alternative products. The traditional analysis suggested that they ranked benefits or disadvantages and reached economically rational decisions based on marginal utility. The emerging marketing approach discussed earlier in Table 6.1 recognizes that consumers undertake risk reduction strategies by seeking out additional information, or in listening to other peoples' advice and experiences as they make their own tourism purchasing decisions. Ultimately, the individual's test of his service experience is his own satisfaction judgement, but it is the sum of all of these which underpins the organization's reputation and its continuing success.

This reinforces Grönroos (2001) who suggests both that the organization should be designed around good service delivery and that its management should focus on quality issues, designing the system from the perspective of its ability to satisfy consumers. Similarly, Chisnall (1985) identified the following twin roles for marketing managers:

1 Interpretation, the analysis and interpretation of behaviour in the market place, both present and projected.
2 Integration, that is, working closely with company colleagues in other functions.

Chisnall argued that marketing is not just concerned with the obvious audiences outside the company; it has an important role to play in adapting attitudes and performance by all company members, that is 'internal selling.' Cowell (1986: 207) has defined the concept in the following way: 'internal marketing means applying the philosophy and practices of marketing to people who serve the external customers so that the best possible people can be employed and retained, and they will do the best possible work.' The implications of internal selling are that the firm recognizes the impact of employees' detailed job decisions on clients' satisfaction, a point which will be considered in more detail later.

Conclusion

This chapter has discussed how managerial decisions on branding, positioning, enhancement to core services, advertising and pricing have consequences for tourists' purchasing behaviour and influence their expectations of service quality. The next chapter investigates what managers can do to improve tourism service systems.

CHAPTER 7

Improving tourism and hospitality service systems

Introduction

Effective managers are always asking questions about what makes their service successful or unsuccessful (Zeithmal, 2000). Noe (1999: Introduction) has stated that 'no greater challenge exists in the marketplace than for a business to be responsible for providing satisfactory tourist and hospitality services'. I suggest in this book that the key is to focus on the service encounter, examining how the service tasks and the service design contribute to the encounter. The delivery system specifies the service to be produced, but as Schmenner (1995: 19) points out, 'it needs to be synchronized with the service task and the service standards so that the service encounter remains a pleasurable one for all concerned'.

Another managerial responsibility is to improve productivity: the way in which the organization uses its resources to create a service. Productivity can be understood as output divided by input (usually stated in money values). This relationship implies that productivity can be improved either by getting more output from the existing level of resources (for example, by reconfiguring a plane from, say, 105 to 120 seats), or reducing input to achieve a given output (for example, by cutting the number of cabin crew to serve 100 passengers from, say, four to three). Both of these approaches to increased financial productivity have potential drawbacks. Regular customers are likely to notice a reduction in seat pitch (leg-room) and the longer wait for meal service during the flight. The amount of work required of staff will also increase in both examples, and beyond a point this may result in staff tiredness, dissatisfaction, and reduced levels of customer service or care. The topic of service productivity includes substitution, waste elimination, reduction of variety and variance, managing demand, and economies of scale, but the focus in this chapter is on the service encounter (Czepiel, Solomon and Surprenant, 1985).

Service management

George and Kelly (1983) have examined the sequence of steps involved in the process of managing services. They identified seven stages, presented in Table 7.1.

It is a consistent theme throughout this book that service experiences are significantly influenced by the interactions between staff and customers. Managerial decisions about the characteristics of the services offered are dependent on the way individual employees interpret service design and performance criteria. Furthermore, service delivery entails interaction with the customer, and its quality therefore depends partly on gaining their cooperation. The view that service quality is produced in the interaction between a customer and elements in the service organization has been referred to as 'interactive quality' (Lehtinen and Lehtinen (1982), cited in Ryan, 1995). However, quality derives not only from the interaction of customers with staff, but also from the way that customers interact with each other. Familiar examples are the difficulty for the courier and the dissatisfaction which all other passengers experience when one client on

Table 7.1 *Steps in managing services*

(1) Orchestrate the encounter
Access: buyer's needs, expectations, knowledge of evaluative criteria
Process: technical expertise, manage interactions, elicit customer participation
Output: satisfying service purchase experience
(2) Quality assessment using established expectations as the basis for judgement
(3) Educate buyers about the unique characteristics of the service
(4) Emphasize organizational image and communicate the image attributes of the firm and its service
(5) Encourage satisfied customers to communicate to others
(6) Recognize contact personnel's role
(7) Involve customers during the design process

Based on George and Kelly (1983)

a coach tour is consistently late in returning to the vehicle after sight-seeing stops, or when a group of people insist on partying energetically late into the night in the hotel room next to yours.

A related problem is that customers' behaviour and perceived attitudes can please or distress staff (Ross, 1993; Bateson, 2002). Because they are directly involved in the production of a service, customers can help and support the people who deliver it, or make it more difficult for staff to carry out their role in the process. An example of supportive behaviour occurs when a passenger, seeing meal service begin in the cabin, lowers his own seat back table, or unfolds it from the armrest. In contrast, other passengers leave this simple task to the cabin staff. Sometimes, a passenger has been seen to object to having to move a game or a computer from the table when the cabin attendant arrives to set it up for meal service. Supportive customer behaviour has been shown to correlate positively with job satisfaction and performance, whereas instrumental behaviour by passengers has negative outcomes for staff.

Instrumental behaviour has been defined as '"telling staff how to perform their tasks". Its dysfunctional results can be minimized by "decoupling" the service, that is, by redesigning it to minimize encounters' (Bowen and Schneider, 1985: 133). However, this approach has been criticized earlier as inappropriate in tourism because it reduces human interactions and responsiveness. Saleh and Ryan (1992) have emphasized the expressive nature of the delivery of the service, that is the ability to empathize with the customer as indicated by their term used in the title of their chapter: 'The conviviality of the service'. From another perspective, since customers have few ways to judge the technical quality of the service, interactions with staff are a primary factor in determining customer satisfaction (Bitner, Booms and Mohr, 1994).

My view is that interaction, consumer satisfaction, the design of the service and the way it is presented are components of the distinction customers make between one company and its competitors. The conclusion to draw from the preceding discussion is not that managers should maximize contact points, increase complexity or invest in the most luxurious service settings. Rather, deliberate decisions should be taken on each of these aspects to create a service balance which is appealing to target customers and which can be delivered by a particular organization reliably and profitably (Yasin and Yavas, 1999).

This chapter focuses particular attention on the interactive aspects of services, where customers and contact staff consume and provide the service. These are widely regarded as important for customers, staff and organizations, as the following quotation indicates.

> The direct contacts between the customer and an employee of the service firm are referred to as the service encounters or moments of truth. These are natural opportunities emerging in the production/delivery process; for example, the interaction between a doctor and a patient, a bank manager and a client, a flight attendant and a passenger. Both the doctor, the bank manager and the flight attendant become part-time marketers: the customer becomes a co producer and a prosumer (the terms pro-ducer and con-sumer as suggested by Toffler, 1980). Looking at it from the opposite angle the term part-time employee can be used to signify the customer's role. If the customer does not cooperate . . . the services cannot be properly produced and delivered. (Gummesson, 1990: 98)

Dyadic and multiplex service interactions

Much of the service literature is concerned with an interaction in which one client is served by one contact person representing the company. Such analyses have traditionally been centred on dyadic interaction at the point of sale (Evans, 1963; Olshavsky, 1973). However, in tourism services the presence of other people sometimes becomes a significant factor in a client's experiences. Service transactions are performed in a public setting. Additionally, the service often affects more than one client, and they interact with each other. Table 7.2 identifies four types of interaction which can occur during service episodes.

Table 7.2 *Interactions during services*

---

(1) service contact staff and customers
(2) interaction between customers
(3) customers and the firm's physical environment
(4) customers and the firm's processes and routines

Based on Bitner, Booms and Tetreault (1990)

During service delivery staff such as those employed in the airtransportation industry have a significant power differential over passengers based on their greater technical knowledge of the complex service delivery technology involved in journeys by air, their company's service design (or blueprint), and its service standards. This differential is significantly emphasized by the style differences between carriers, which means that passengers who have had experience of one airline, type of service or class might have misperceptions of another airline's practices. Furthermore, as Figure 7.1 indicates, from the client's perspective, he or she is passing through a series of service events, but the staff member provides a particular service on a repetitive basis. This point escalates in significance when routine service delivery is disrupted and passengers demand or expect particular responses to their own needs, or when they complain formally after such an occurrence.

Customer participation in services

A complicating factor is that passengers have differing expectations of the service.

> Customer expectations and requests that exceed the firm's ability to perform account for 74% of the reported communications difficulties. This implies that . . . even if the system is working at optimal efficiency, employees can expect to face a large number of communications difficulties. (Nyquist, Bitner and Booms, 1985: 207)

The authors went on to identify nine service situations likely to cause problems for staff, summarized in Table 7.3.

Table 7.3 *Difficulties in dealing with customers*

(1)   unreasonable demands
(2)   demands against policy
(3)   unacceptable treatment of employees
(4)   drunkenness
(5)   breaking social norms
(6)   special needs customers (psychological, language or medical difficulties)
(7)   unavailable service
(8)   unacceptably slow performance
(9)   unacceptable service

Based on Nyquist, Bitner and Booms (1985)

The foregoing discussion of service design has given additional emphasis to the role of contact staff in the satisfaction of clients. A complex service such as that provided during airtravel or in a hotel is often designed to be delivered by several teams of people, each with specialized but separated skills such as check-in or in-flight service. The service management model proposed by George and Kelly discussed above therefore has to be enlarged to accommodate issues involved in the coordination and management of work teams. Many organizations have implemented programmes to help staff understand the ways in which their particular role contributes to the overall success of the enterprise. Lockwood *et al.* (1992: 328) have described how one hotel put on a programme called 'Together we care'. They comment: 'the company realised that, although together they might have cared, individually nobody gave a damn!' The significance of this has been underlined by Bitner, Booms and Tetreault (1990: 71):

> Many times . . . interaction *is* the service from the customer's point of view yet front line employees are not trained to understand customers and do not have the freedom and discretion needed to relate to customers in ways that ensure effective service.

Service encounters

It is worth re-emphasizing the effect on tourists' satisfaction of their interactions with the staff of an airline, airport, hotel and other companies supplying facilities for their holiday. This concern with service encounters reflects other writers' views. 'Since service encounters are the consumer's main source of information for conclusions regarding quality and service differentiation, no marketer can afford to leave the service encounter to chance' (Shostack, 1985: 243). Similarly, Adams (1976) noted that 'service contact staff often feel as close to their customers psychologically and physically as to their colleagues. They are the organization's most immediate interface with the customer.'

These interactive aspects of service encounters are significant at a more fundamental level: interactions with other people are basic human activities, and occupy a large part of our time. Poor service encounter experiences affect the quality of everyday life, and staff might spend their entire working day in repeated service encounters with customers who might already be dissatisfied by some incident which occurred earlier. It does not even have to be a problem directly related to the service provided by a particular firm, as was indicated in the first case study in this book, which described the problems that could arise for people in Edinburgh making their way to the airport by bus.

Mention has been made of the complexity of tourism services, often comprising a large number of components or process steps and involving several service providers. Gummesson (1993) has contrasted the customer's perspective of using a variety of services in a serial or linear fashion with the repetition and greater process familiarity of contact staff. This is illustrated in Figure 7.1, which demonstrates that staff working in one phase of the service deal with a large number of customers, while from the point of view of a particular client what is important is the way in which a series of specialized activities contribute to the overall service. There are both technical and service features to each part encounter, but the significance of this model is that while staff become very familiar with their special roles, the customer can experience the service as a number of fragmented activities delivered in differing ways.

Taken together, this discussion demonstrates that the nature of the service interface, and the quality of contact between clients and staff, can enhance or detract from:

1. achieving customer satisfaction
2. achieving staff satisfaction
3. accomplishing the organization's mission

From the perspective of competitive marketing, an improved understanding of customers' participation in service events yields insights on how to manage those services to their greater satisfaction. This may have two beneficial effects: it is likely to promote customer loyalty by encouraging repeat purchases from satisfied customers, and may contribute to more refined positioning through product adjustment, client awareness and advertising appeals. But the issue that arises, as was noted earlier, is which aspects of service performance should be measured.

Davidson, Sweeney and Stampfl (1988) pointed out that the secret of success in a service industry is recognition that customer-contact personnel are the key people in the organization. The level of analysis

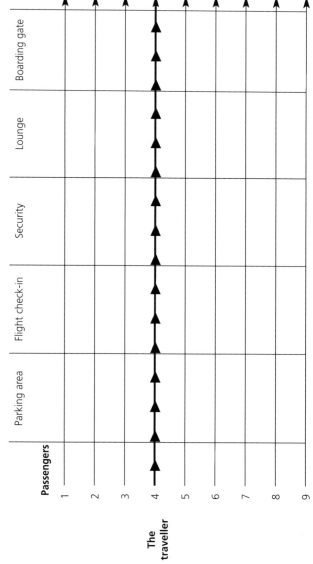

Figure 7.1 *Routes for passengers and staff through airport processes: complexity and repetition (based on Gummesson, 1993)*

for marketers should include the transaction between the company, its staff and the clients. Lalonde and Zinzser (1976) found an emphasis in the empirical literature on the significance of 'the buyer/seller interface'. Czepiel, Solomon and Surprenant (1985) used the term 'Service Encounter' (SE) for this interface. Table 7.4 lists seven points distinguishing SE roles from other interpersonal transactions:

Table 7.4 *Service encounters (SEs)*

---

(1) SEs are purposeful
(2) SEs are work, recognized as such by both parties
(3) SEs are a special type of stranger relationship
(4) SEs are limited in scope: they are focused by and limited by the functional requirements to areas of legitimate enterprise
(5) Information exchanges in the SE are limited to task-related matters
(6) The roles of both the client and the service staff are well defined
(7) During the service there is a temporary status differential between the client and the server

---

Based on Czepiel, Solomon and Surprenant (1985)

The service encounter is a process in which people do things together, continuously interpreting the situation and adjusting to each other. Much of the interaction, however, is guided by rules which are largely unrecognized until something goes wrong. In other words, to paraphrase Czepiel and his co-authors, staff and client join in a dyad for the express purpose of creating a service. In doing so they each adopt situation-specific roles and behaviour. The framework for these purposeful roles is provided by management decisions determining the service delivery system, and it is this system which distinguishes the outcomes for consumers and staff of one organization's market offering from those of its competitors (Bettencourt, 1997). The lines of reasoning summarized above led Shostack (1985) to argue that:

- the encounter can be controlled; and
- it can be enhanced.

Service performance: further discussion

One strategy which managers often adopt in their search for consistent service is to minimize employee discretion and judgement whenever possible (Sasser, Olsen and Wycoff, 1978). As noted previously, this approach works well in the manufacturing sector and may also be quite effective for 'low contact' services (Chase, 1978), although the study of a pizza company in Case study 4.5 (above) has shown that this view can be challenged. The strategy of minimizing employee discretion relies on the specification of tasks to a standard of performance required by management, thereby providing a basis for measuring the effectiveness of staff performing tasks. Increased standardization implies a reduction in the discretion allowed to individual employees; however, this contradicts service sector clients' normal expectations of being treated as individuals, with needs that differ from those of other clients, and which may vary during the many events of which a service is composed. Efficiency goals may have the benefit of efficient use of resources and clarification of performance targets for staff, but the resultant mechanical style of service can conflict with the customers' expectations of warm and friendly service. Underlying this discussion are the twin assumptions that consumers experience a service as a series of events, while managers see the service as a set of elements which require skilled coordination, and resource control, in delivering specified standards to clients.

The service performance is experiential, and as it involves the way in which a customer participates, he or she has the potential to help or hinder the process. The view that service quality is produced in the interaction between a customer and elements in the service organization has been referred to as 'interactive quality'. Supportive customer behaviour has been shown to correlate positively with job satisfaction and performance, whereas instrumental behaviour by passengers has negative outcomes for staff. Hjalager (2001) has argued that it is beneficial to involve clients more directly in their service, empowering them to contribute more effectively to the way it functions and so improving their satisfaction with it.

There is often more to the ways in which tourists 'participate' in the services they purchase than a passive acquiescence in the service delivery system, or an occasional dispute with staff or managers when some error occurs. The point at which a customer interacts with the organization has been recognized as a major organizational design variable (Chase and Tansik, 1983; Yasin and Yavas, 1999). Part of the problem is that services are delivered by people to other people, and this makes the staff – their appearance, attitudes, competencies and behaviour towards the customer, towards each other, and towards their employer – a significant factor in the service experienced by a customer (Shostack, 1985). Another major factor is that task uncertainty is greater when staff work in direct contact with clients. The interaction creates uncertainty for service employees primarily because clients' behaviour cannot be accurately predicted, yet staff have to communicate and interact with customers in performing their work. But in services, the significance of effective interactions goes beyond delivery; it seems that the ability of workers to notice and understand customers' desires and respond to them appropriately is crucial (Solomon *et al.*, 1982). Similarly, Weitz (1981) demonstrated that sales representatives who modify their approach contingent upon customers behaviour are more effective than those who do not. Shepherd (1999) has confirmed that salespeople's responsiveness to customers can confer a competitive advantage.

The Servuction approach

The term 'servuction' has been coined for the involvement of customers in the production of service (Eiglier and Langeard, 1987).

> Servuction refers to the production and delivery of services – the word is easily recognized as analogous to production. The word emphasises an essential fact: services are different from products and should not be forced to borrow terminology from manufacturing. (Gummesson, 1990: 97)

The real difference is the fact that the customer is involved in servuction processes, therefore the 'service provider has less control over the environment and the behaviour of the actors' (ibid.). Gummesson asks how the quality of cars would be affected if customers were allowed to wander around the factory.

> In participating in the servuction the customer helps – or makes difficult – the process. Consequently, servuction quality is partly the result of interaction and joint efforts between the customer and the service provider; it is a result of the division of labour. (Ibid.)

In consumerist gap terms, if any of the moments of truth fail, a consumerist gap has been opened, causing dissatisfaction. The result of any customer dissatisfaction is twofold for the organization: the costs of complaint handling, and the potential loss of future business both from the distressed customers and from others to whom they voice their dissatisfaction (Fornell and Wernerfelt, 1987). Management discovers its failure to provide satisfaction by two feedback mechanisms: exit and voice. Voice occurs when a consumer expresses dissatisfaction directly to the firm. Hirschman (1986) has classified customers as alert or inert. Alert customers exit when they experience dissatisfaction; inert customers voice, but may exit. Exit is a corrective market mechanism which should affect the firm's decision making. Successful firms are sensitive to exit!

Many of the models of marketing behaviour include a feedback loop (or loops), a mechanism by which consumers are able to express their opinions of a current market offering. The function is to allow the producer to modify future output to obtain a closer match to customers' wishes. The complaining customer attempts directly to change the firm's policies or behaviour, or to obtain compensation. Voice is more desirable than exit!

Quality control

Another significant factor distinguishing services from manufactured goods is the relative difficulty of developing and implementing effective quality control programmes. The quality standards developed and implemented by a tourism organization's managers are significant to the consumer's satisfaction in two critical ways, as indicated in Table 7.5.

Service standards

Underlying the investigation of the meaning to customers of their experiences is a view that this is useful to managers in developing a

Table 7.5 *Issues in tourism quality standards*

(1)	The level of service which management sets might be higher (or lower) than the client's anticipation of service standards
(2)	Quality systems might not control service standards in ways which matter to clients

competitive position and then maintaining the advantages gained. In essence, this book argues that an understanding of customer perceptions of service delivery is a necessary but insufficient condition for the effective management of consumer experiences. Equally important (but a secondary focus here) is an understanding of the organizational and technical realities which underlie the service design or blueprint. But the blueprint for service enactment is drawn up in the context of two constraints. The general technical and regulatory factors under which businesses operate are the first constraint. Secondly, the blueprint for two companies operating in similar circumstances will differ, reflecting the corporate mission statement and its senior managers' understanding of the contingencies and conditions of a particular period. Many organizations attempt to measure service quality, but 'they look primarily at the end results . . . and tend to neglect the service components contributing to those end results' (Senior and Akehurst, 1992: 177). Similarly, the co-editors of a benchmark study of service system interactions identified in their preface an overriding question for those who manage or research service industries: 'What makes a service encounter good – good for the employee, good for the customer and good for the firm?' (Czepiel, Solomon and Surprenant, 1985).

From the perspective of the service paradigm discussed in this book, the first step in quality control should be to acknowledge whose judgement or evaluation of quality is pivotal to the actions then taken to ensure that quality is delivered. Longer term, quality management is the key to continuing success as it embraces the view underlying the service quality dynamics model that customers' expectations of service standards are not static over time. Based on their experience with competitor or substitute suppliers, customers expect that the current performance of a service organization will be superior to their previous experience of it.

Quality control in tourism services

The foregoing discussion raises the issue of what managers should monitor (Johnson, Tsiros and Lancioni, 1995; Dickey, 1998). What is measured traditionally is process standards such as the time taken to serve a client, use of resources, or the progress of the client through the events which constitute the service. This emphasis on process is essential but it is not sufficient; what matters also is the outcome. Few organizations have the courage to empower contact staff to take responsibility for their own customers' satisfaction, and few managers are willing to recognize the problems they may create or implement for staff trying to serve clients well. If customer resistance to service styles is not recognized, understood and acted on, or if minor customer complaints are not treated with respect, the outcome is reduced customer satisfaction, compared with what might have been. This creates an opportunity for more responsive competitors to redefine the vision of service in that sector. However, many organizations focus more on the technical, predefined service criteria which are relatively easy to monitor and control. The International Standards Organization (ISO) can be seen as bolstering this approach.

ISO 9000

The quality management research presented in this book is concerned with understanding how the organization's processes contribute to (or detract from) customer enjoyment. The ISO 9000 approach is rather different in purpose although some of its methods are similar to those discussed here. The ISO method is based on documenting the company's processes. The ISO test is whether, if a catastrophe decimated its staff, it would be possible for the company to recreate its processes based on its ISO records. This concept is heavily criticized for the paperwork it generates (Vine and Hele; 1998), but the fundamental weakness is that it does little to enhance actual quality (Dale et al., 1994), despite some recognition in the specifications. Nevertheless, it is being widely adopted partly because in many countries firms bidding for government contracts are required to hold ISO certification. Another rationale might be that ISO has demonstrated that it is feasible to implement quality control in service organizations.

Certification is introduced to guarantee consistent quality from certified suppliers (Trent and Monczka, 1999). They pointed out that suppliers are becoming receptive to a standard set of requirements, such as ISO 9000 standards, and that over 90% of larger firms expected to apply some level of ISO 9000 standards to their supplier assessment practices by 2000. ISO guidelines state that the 'design of the service specification and the service delivery system are interdependent and interact throughout the design . . . flow charts are a useful method to depict all activities, relationships and interdependencies' (ISO 9004-2, 1990: 15). Table 7.6 summarizes some of the main sections of the Australian Guidelines to services (Standards Australia, 1990).

Table 7.6 *ISO service elements*

Section 5.2.3	Primary goals for establishing quality should include: • customer satisfaction consistent with professional standards and ethics • continuous improvement of service • consideration of society and environment • efficiency in providing the service
Section 5.2.4	• A quality system structure is required to control, evaluate and improve service quality throughout all stages of the provision of a service • Responsibility and authority should be explicitly defined for all personnel whose activities influence service quality • A management representative should be designated responsible for ensuring that the quality system is established, audited, continually measured and reviewed for improvement
Section 5.4.3	All service elements, requirements and provisions incorporated in the quality system should be defined and documented within: • a quality manual • a quality plan • procedures • quality records

Based on Standards Australia (1990)

Quality audits

Another important approach is to audit service systems for quality.

> A quality audit is a systematic appraisal of service quality. It offers a quick and effective means of assessing service quality from the point of view of the customer. . . . Quality audits have often been conducted by inhouse personnel, particularly in large organizations such as hotel chains. However, inhouse auditors quickly become familiar with the service standards of their organization. They may take some aspects of the service for granted and will also tend to emphasize the aspects of quality which management regard as important rather than those which are significant to the customer. (Johns and Clark, 1993: 360)

These authors have developed a method of tracing the customer's service experience as a journey through a series of events. Discussing museum service auditing they identify the features noted in Table 7.7.

Table 7.7 *Features of museum service quality*

- extensive movement of people
- unpredictable flow and demand patterns
- a need to help customers make decisions about what they want to see and in what detail
- a comparatively long journey time during which services such as food, drink and toilet facilities will probably be needed
- commercial opportunities

Based on Johns and Clark (1993)

Profit impacts of service quality control measures

Noe (1999) has summarized the consensus of many researchers who argue that service quality and satisfaction result in increased profitability and occupancy rates for customer-oriented firms. Buzzell and Gale (1987: 7) have stressed the importance of understanding and meeting consumers' service quality perceptions:

> There is no doubt that relative perceived quality and profitability are strongly related. Whether the profit measure is return on sales or return on investment, businesses with a superior product/service offering clearly outperform those with inferior quality.

Gummesson advocated service blueprinting as a systematic way of describing a service in order to make sure that all elements are included, so that their cost and contribution to revenue in the composition of the service can be examined. Gummesson (1990) has identified two ways to improve profit through quality measures:

- Improved market performance leads to increased sales and increasing market share (or decreased price elasticity). Increased quality ultimately enables the price to be raised.
- A reduction in defects leads to lower unit costs of production and the costs of servicing complainants is also lower.

Zeithmal, Berry and Parasuraman (1996: 31) report that many organizations 'have instituted measurement and management approaches to improve their service. . . . the issue of highest priority today involves understanding the impact of service quality on profit and other financial outcomes of the organization.' However, they go on to point out that 'the link between service quality and profits is neither straightforward nor clear'. Hollins and Hollins (1991) have also advocated a process of continuous improvements, relying on a belief that the service is a chain of events which the customer experiences – a view that also underlies service blueprinting. They regard the stage of designing the service as its managers' main opportunity to determine the characteristics of the service offered to customers. Dwyer, Murray and Mott (1998) describe continuous improvement in hospitality organizations, defining it as incremental improvements to a company's processes led by the Chief Executive Officer (CEO) and managerial commitment to organizational learning, and seen by all employees as an integral part of their work role. The implications of this are considered in Chapter 8.

Service problem or service crisis?

Dissatisfaction with some elements of a complex service is probably a common occurrence in the tourism industry. In most cases, a service problem is not immediately a service crisis, although it may escalate into one: Basil Fawlty knew intuitively how to exacerbate his clients' and staff's concerns, as John Cleese has demonstrated to the enjoyment of TV audiences around the world. In contrast, a real-world example of how problems can be overcome to the satisfaction of everyone involved was documented when a group of ornithologists experienced several serious difficulties during a visit to Venezuela. One flight was missed when their bus broke down, their leader and guide were left behind for another flight, and twice their hotel was changed. 'About 20 people made the trip, how many were satisfied? Surprise! At the end, all spoke of what a great trip it had been and were enthusiastic at the prospect of a future expedition' (Swan and Bowers, 1998: 59).

Fornell and Wernerfelt (1987) reported that in over half the cases which they investigated by following up written complaints, employees' responses to the situation had aggravated the complaint. This is significant because an even greater proportion of complainants reported that they would tell others about the events when their complaint was unresolved. However, in only a few cases was there a need for financial compensation; it was more likely that the complainant wanted better communications and a more pleasant response to his problem.

There are three main phases to dealing with service problems, as was indicated in Figure 3.4 (Chapter 3). The immediate challenge is to recognize that a problem has occurred. The response should be to remedy the defect promptly and without drama. A clean fork can easily be substituted for a dirty one. But the defect is a service problem too. This is addressed first by waiters who respond to the client, perhaps spending extra time with the customer or by suggesting an addition to the meal ordered, offering it on a complimentary basis if they have the authority to do so. The third phase is normally the responsibility of managers rather than contact staff, although some are empowered to offer compensation such as an upgrade, a glass of cognac or a voucher discounting any future purchase. Beyond that, and importantly, the organization can learn from the customer's experience (Brown, Cowles and Tuten, 1996; McCollough, Berry and Yavas, 2000; Miller, Craighead and Karwan, 2000).

Learning from complaints

Lewis and Morris (1987) have distinguished between individual complaint handling – determined by the long-term value of future purchases of an individual complainant and that person's word of mouth impact upon other consumers – and aggregate complaint analysis – identifying and resolving common consumer problems thus avoiding their recurrence, and typically calling for a change in the firm's marketing mix.

One of the most significant recent supplier responses to consumer discontent has been the widespread establishment within firms of formal organizational structures to deal specifically with consumer affairs. Typically, consumer affairs departments seek to improve relations with the consuming public and to make firms more responsive to the needs and grievances of consumers. They have the potential to improve the satisfaction of consumers in the marketplace, and offer significant opportunities for increasing marketing effectiveness by improving the company's knowledge of its customers' service experiences and expectations. A report for the US Commission of Consumer Affairs (TARP, 1979) showed that complaining customers exhibit stronger brand loyalty than customers who did not complain and that loyalty could be strengthened further by the firm's complaint handling.

Complaints are not always directed formally to the organization supplying a service. Many customers, whether dissatisfied or pleased with a service, discuss their experiences with friends, relatives or colleagues. The significance of word of mouth communications in social interactions is that dissatisfied customers are likely to tell many friends and business colleagues about their (perceived) bad experiences (Stafford, 1966). They may thereby influence their contacts away from that supplier. However, if the dissatisfied passenger can be persuaded to direct his or her complaint to the airline, the company then has a second chance to put matters right, and in addition to placating one customer (and his or her travelling party), may also gain favourable word of mouth recommendations among the passenger's circle of influence. Reliance on customers' unsolicited comments is subject to limitations, such as those identified by Lewis and Morris (1987). They pointed to differences in personal behavioural characteristics tending to make complaints more or less likely, and addressed the organizational consequences of customer complaints, suggesting that interdepartmental communications might be suppressed because of various behavioural barriers in particular organizations. In particular, the higher the rate of consumer complaints, the more isolated is the complaint handling function likely to become.

The value of complaints lies both in their power as a communications device and as a means of giving the firm a chance to turn a dissatisfied customer into a satisfied and loyal customer (Fornell and Wernerfelt, 1987). The foregoing analysis suggests that marketing-oriented managers should encourage complaining behaviour; but the key to long-term benefits from the strategy lie in effective analytical techniques as a basis to their response strategies, and a willingness by the organization to learn.

Service interruptions

Delays are an operational hazard for transport companies, arising from mechanical failure, absence of key staff, congestion, the weather and other problems. As this book was being completed, the European Union was planning to introduce a standard compensation tariff for delayed air passengers (but not those travelling by rail or bus, or caught up in road congestion). Most transport companies have detailed contingency plans to deal with the operational problems that may occasionally occur as a result of the complex nature of their service. Managerial effort in the face of an operational delay often concentrates on the technical (Type A) tasks needed to restore normal service. But a further type of managerial skill is required to overcome all the effects of an interrupted service. Type B responses are concerned with the management of clients' experiences during the interruption. Successful Type B management responses depend on an awareness of customers' needs during a service interruption, and of the problems which customer-contact staff face (see Chapter 3 for a fuller discussion). These staff act as mediators of company policy; they form the channels of communication for information about the interruption and enable clients to make their needs known to the company. Contact staff therefore perform a crucial role in their company's market performance (Nyquist, Bitner and Booms, 1985; Gummesson, 1990; Sparks, 2002).

The core product for an airline is safe and timely transport between the passenger's point of origin and his or her destination. Research at Lockheed, the American aircraft manufacturer, took this line and resulted in a Traffic Flow Model (TFM) which placed a monetary value on journey times. A related perspective regards time spent on the journey as a disutility, or displacement. In a perfect world (for travellers) perfect service might be defined as 'a non-stop jet departing at every instant from each point to all others'. In this scenario the total trip time is the non-stop jet time. Eriksen and Liu (1979: 17), in a study for NASA – the American space agency, have described the situation in our imperfect world: 'The total trip time is the sum of the actual travel time including stops and connections, and the amount of time the traveller is displaced from where he wishes to travel to by schedule inconveniences.'

The NASA study discussed many 'schedule inconveniences' including airports remote from a traveller's point of origin or his or her destination, changes of plane en route, and so on. These displacements are an inevitable result of the compromises which managers have to take in designing services under particular constraints, but a further and more distressing time displacement results from unplanned delays. Delays vary in their causes, duration, scale, and impact on airline operations, on passengers and staff.

Understanding passenger expectations during delay management

Maister (1985) has pointed out that the experience of waiting for service (in contrast to the mathematical theory of queues) has been somewhat neglected. He has also argued that anxiety makes waiting seem longer, unexplained waits seem longer than those where an explanation has been given, and 'once the flight is over, waiting to get out when there is no more utility to be received is aggravating' (ibid.: 122).

The starting point for a consumerist gap analysis is the technical problem giving rise to a delay. A typical cause is the failure of some component to meet its test criteria prior to take-off, resulting in the captain's decision to rectify the problem before proceeding. Passengers are often critical of airlines for these technical delays, and less frequently they voice a lack of confidence in particular aircraft or engines, notably after a recent accident involving that type, as occurred with the DC10 shortly after it was introduced into service. In contrast, analysis of customer correspondence suggests that most passengers accept and support their captain's decision not to proceed in such circumstances. This can be interpreted as recognition of the safety aspects, and professional behaviour on the part of the captain. In itself, the announcement of a technical delay can be regarded as contributing to confidence, but not satisfaction.

The management of passengers during such a delay was a main focus of interest in my early consumerist gap research. Any service interruption which occurs depresses satisfaction below the level anticipated, and a consumerist gap has opened. Accordingly, each event during a service interruption is assessed as either boosting or depressing satisfaction, and an explanation of the causative factors was sought from passengers' reports. An extension of the study is concerned with the way in which managers respond to a delay. As noted above, two types of managerial effort are then required to bridge this gap: Type A responses coordinate the technical resources and skills needed to restore the service, and are beyond the scope of a consumerist gap study; Type B responses are concerned with restoring the customers' satisfaction by attending to their comfort and individual needs.

CASE STUDY 7.1

A long flight delay

Delays to flights are a depressingly common feature of travellers' experiences, and these occurrences also result in problems for airlines, their staff and other organizations involved in the service, such as airports and airtraffic control. The study was based on a content analysis of passenger correspondence to the airline resulting from this incident. The passengers' accounts were then discussed with an expert management group.

One passenger wrote to the airline's CEO stating that he is a frequent flyer on the airline, using its premium business class. He gave the flight number and date, and stated that about an hour after take-off from a North American airport for an overnight transatlantic flight, the Captain announced that he was returning as a precautionary measure because an engine malfunction warning light had illuminated in the cockpit display.

Some time after the plane landed dinner was served on board. Eventually, the baggage was unloaded and they were taken to the down town Sheraton where the accommodation was comfortable and the meals were good. His opinion was 'so far so good'. Although no airline staff contacted the group, the local airline staff handled the situation well, but they had not provided much information.

The following day, passengers were given a series of departure times. They boarded buses at one time, but were unloaded. 'A group of 300 passengers did not know what was happening, and anger erupted.' Eventually they were returned to the airport, at midnight, 26 hours after the scheduled take-off. Elderly passengers were exhausted, and small children had become fractious.

There were no trolleys or porters, and again no airline representatives were there; it was left to other airlines' staff to sort out the mess. 'An enterprising management would have been on hand to supervise and accept the bottled up wrath.' The procedures were very slow at the airport. There were no executive lounge facilities although other airlines have them there. Other airlines (three named) compare very favourably with this one. This passenger concluded his letter by stating that in future, he is likely to fly this route with a competitor.

Other correspondents largely confirmed the sequence of events. However, economy passengers complained that they had been disembarked soon after the plane landed, although there were no catering facilities available to them in the lounge because the airport had shut down for the night. The few staff on duty had been hastily recalled, and actually worked for a competing airline which was based in that airport. There was also some disagreement over details such as the number of times on which departure had been delayed from the hotel. The main causes of dissatisfaction are summarized in Table 7.8.

Management review of delay
Five airline managers participated in a detailed review of the analysis of the correspondence as a preliminary step to drawing up a report. The meeting was scheduled for two hours over a light lunch, and lasted for a few minutes longer. Following a brief introduction by the researcher, each participant was handed a synopsis of one correspondent's complaint, and 77 excerpts from other correspondents arranged under the general headings noted in Table 7.8.

Participants were asked to discuss how typical this incident was

Table 7.8 *Sources of dissatisfaction during a long delay*

- *Discomfort*, particularly for economy passengers who had to wait in the airport lounge rather than on board the plane and who were transferred to the hotel after premium class passengers
- *Personal consequences* for each passenger of the delay, for example missing a business appointment or urgent family matters
- *Attitudes and behaviour of staff*, both of the airline and other organizations
- *Effects of limited or wrong information* and the control over passengers exercised during the delay
- *Contact with home*
- *Awareness that other passengers were being treated differently*
- *Lack of offers to reroute passengers*

---

of major delays when they occur. The views expressed on this were that although each incident has particular characteristics, and each correspondent has individual concerns or complaints, the analysis of this delay had isolated representative problems for consideration.

Much of the session was devoted to a discussion in which the 77 excerpts were subjected to scrutiny. The objective was to focus on the interpretation of events by passengers, with the intention of establishing the effect on customer satisfaction of managerial actions following the delay.

At several points in the session, aspects of passengers' comments which had not been clear to the researcher were explained by participating managers. These included the many implied requests for compensation which were not quantified. It emerged that this is a common problem and customers often feel that the airline should propose a suitable amount of compensation. Secondly, reference by passengers to the airline's advertising slogans which emphasized its reliability and the high standards of attention to customers' personal needs was considered by the expert group to be typical. This finding tends to confirm one of the main points underpinning service quality theory: that clients evaluate their experiences against the satisfaction they had anticipated.

Several possible steps which an airline could take to reduce the discomfort or stress experienced by delayed passengers were discussed in the context of the correspondence reviewed. Benefits and costs were outlined for providing specific facilities, such as telephone calls home, rerouting and a personal apology on arrival by senior managers. The discretion of contact staff and their high degree of influence on passengers was discussed, including problems of staff briefing, cost control, staffing levels and interpersonal relations between staff and passengers, including differences of race, age and sex.

The airline managers provided technical explanations for creeping delays. It can often be difficult to assess an engineering problem, which becomes more complex as deeper diagnosis is made. A replacement part may prove defective, or further checks may be considered prudent. But the consequence is that passengers are in limbo, waiting ready to depart but unable to take advantage of the local facilities. If the airline releases them, it may not be able to reassemble the group for departure within available flight slots or the crew's hours. Several passengers' remarks appear to support the view that they were aware of these problems, but found them frustrating none the less.

From a satisfaction management (quality of service) perspective, a trade-off between the operational constraint on passengers of having them prepared to depart, and setting a highly probable target time for departure might be advantageous, in freeing them of spatial and time limits to a reasonable extent. Against this, the airline's operating manual has to be drawn up in recognition of the potential costs of missing the revised departure slot.

Figure 7.2 is based on the management discussions about this delay. It shows how various responses improved customers' feelings about the delay while others exacerbated the situation.

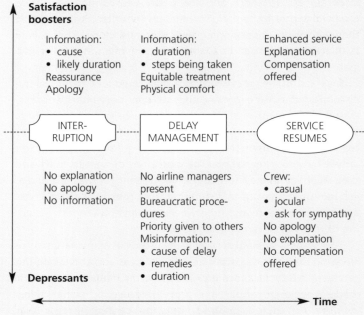

Figure 7.2 *Satisfaction management during a delay*

Discussion

The foregoing example indicates that most travellers are willing to make allowances for the vagaries of a journey, particularly when weather or technical problems are evidently the cause of a delay. However, responses to a delay require more than the correction of technical problems. Knowledge of the problems which clients themselves experience, and an understanding of their reactions, can assist in refining and improving the design of the service recovery approaches adopted towards passengers. This can be gained by requesting clients' comments and opinions (Lewis and Morris, 1987) or, as shown above, by analysing their unsolicited comments. An understanding of their own perceptions of events is important in improving future handling of problems such as lengthy delays, because the way in which staff respond to problems can either attenuate or exacerbate the client's initial disappointments. Recognition of the problem, an apology and a solution usually restore satisfaction to normal levels, and an extra gesture in recompense may boost satisfaction even higher. In contrast, if the client himself has to initiate remedial action by complaining about a problem, it is less likely that management responses will restore his satisfaction to the level anticipated prior to the service, and the consumerist gap acid test will not have been passed. In the highly competitive market for airline travel, frequent occurrences of this situation have the potential to damage the airline's future viability.

The costs of quality control

Three sets of costs are involved in quality control systems, shown in Table 7.9. It is a managerial responsibility and prerogative to decide which of these should be emphasized in the company's service strategy.

An organization incurs costs from any service failure, but implementing a quality control system also entails costs. These costs relate to actions taken to get a service right from the start, auditing that it is correctly delivered and the expenses of responding to any failure (Lockyer and Oakland, 1981). From a managerial perspective, the techniques used in service blueprinting and consumerist gap studies can assist in locating problems with an existing service delivery

Table 7.9 *Costs of quality management*

Costs	Examples
Failure costs	Errors, correction, checking, dealing with customers complaints, the costs of getting it wrong
Appraisal costs	Checking, inspection, quality audits, checking that it is right
Prevention costs	Planning training, good procedures, getting it right first time

Lockyer and Oakland (1981)

system, and it can also be helpful in evaluating the benefits of alternative remedial actions. Apart from the physical or psychological consequences for customers and staff of unsatisfactory services, the costs include disturbance in the running of departments, and a reduction in future sales levels, resulting from dissatisfaction. Further costs are incurred in implementing preventative measures to reduce future dissatisfaction, including the redesign of service delivery systems or training and motivational programmes for staff.

Another important factor is the informal communications between individuals concerning their evaluation of service experiences, particularly in response to problems (Saxby *et al.*, 2000). Anderson (1998) considers that the individual's degree of satisfaction is generally regarded as the antecedent of their product-related comments to colleagues. He further notes that there is a general consensus that satisfied and loyal customers engage in comment, but also empirical evidence indicates that dissatisfied customers are more vocal still.

As Bateson (1995: 65) notes: 'When service failures occur, the organization's response has the potential to either restore customer satisfaction and reinforce customer loyalty or exacerbate the situation and drive customers to a competing firm.' Fisk, Brown and Bitner (1993: 75) regard service recovery, the actions the organization takes in response to a service failure, as a research area of great importance: 'The service recovery paradox predicts that a customer's cumulative satisfaction with a service organization . . . will increase when he or she is very satisfied with the organization's handling of a service failure.'

Conclusion

Once a service has been designed, managers face the challenges of ensuring that it is delivered to clients in a way which is consistent yet recognizes their individual needs and concerns. They must also respond to service problems as and when they arise.

This chapter has demonstrated how the consumerist gap method focuses on customer satisfaction as the dependent variable, an individual outcome heavily influenced by service encounters, service technology and the management philosophy. By examining the factors influencing passengers' changing satisfaction, another measure of the effectiveness of any quality control systems in place can be activated, and the benefits of additional quality control systems assessed. The appropriateness of the technical design of delivery systems can also be explored, and together with an under-standing of the meaning to customers of their experiences, is helpful to managers seeking to develop a competitive position and to then maintain the advantages gained.

The concluding chapter of this book turns attention to a topic which has been raised several times, that is the skills, attitudes and approaches needed to manage tourism service organizations effectively.

CHAPTER 8

The management of tourism and hospitality organizations

Introduction

There is a general consensus in the research community that tourism services are complex, and that any aspect can contribute to the success or failure of a service. In earlier chapters, I noted that despite this, much management action and many studies are hindered by inappropriate ways of thinking about services, and their complex nature. The 'first generation' approach to services discussed by Normann (1991) persists, relying on experience transferred from the manufacturing sector where management decisions about design and manufacturing control usually result in logically predictable outcomes. The weakness in the management and analysis of service organizations arises from themes in economic theory which rely on mathematical analysis of a set of forces tending to stability and equilibrium, in contrast to the heterogeneous, dynamic forces tending to greater diversity and increasing complexity in the marketplace (Faulkner and Russell, 1997; Gleick, 1987). These are inadequate to either describe or analyse tourism service quality issues fully, and imply that flexible, innovative management approaches are needed. This chapter now considers improvements to the management of tourism and hospitality organizations as a framework for the analysis of service design and delivery presented in preceding chapters.

First or second generation service thinking

Marketing insights and methods play a central role in setting organizational resources to work towards achieving predetermined targets of turnover, growth, volume of business and so on. Organizational targets, and the steps to reach them, are usually specified in a business plan which shows how the organization intends to satisfy its objectives. These may be set out in a formal statement of its mission, the way in which it relates to society, and reflect intelligence about emerging trends in the company's environment, as well as a detailed understanding of the company's own operational strengths.

Mattsson (1985) distinguished two types of relationship essential to a firm's success: vertical relationships describe the relation between a firm and its customers; horizontal relations exist between a firm and others supplying it. Porter (1985) stressed the importance of sound industry relationships; Buhalis and Laws (2001) have edited a collection of studies examining key aspects of channel management in the tourism and hospitality industry. More recently, research has focused on the special management characteristics of service organizations, particularly service encounters, service design, service quality and customer satisfaction, internal marketing and relationship marketing. Together, they represent a new approach to management which Gummesson (1990) argued is sufficiently different from earlier approaches to merit recognition as a paradigm shift.

A great deal of managerial effort is directed towards achieving improvements in the efficiency and effectiveness of organizations. It was noted earlier that one of the distinguishing characteristics of services is their dependence on direct contact between staff and clients in the delivery of the service. In contrast, the manufacturing of most products occurs 'offstage', remote from the view of customers. Although managers may wish to specify precise standards for their services, just as a production manager in a factory setting would be expected to, in reality each service transaction is itself a variable, and the quality of the service is dependent on the interaction between staff and client in the context of the physical setting and the technical features of the service delivery system designed by its managers. Furthermore, the quality of the service provided is judged by each client. This suggests both that the organization should be designed around good service delivery and that its management should be constantly focused on quality issues, designing the system from that perspective, as Feigenbaum (1956) suggested.

An additional factor in many services is that the variety of tasks involved calls for a team-based approach. Consequently, it has been pointed out that 'team work is the focus of service quality programmes in several firms known for their outstanding customer service' (Garvin, 1988). Wisner (1999) studied transportation quality improvement programmes, and placed importance on finding the root causes of quality problems, employee empowerment, and setting quality goals and standards. He showed that it is effective for managers to involve and support employees in a continuous improvement process and to stress the importance of role behaviours that allow the programmes to succeed. Wisner also noted a strong correlation between quality programmes and performance elements such as customer service, on-time deliveries, competitiveness, customer complaints, future growth expectations, employee productivity and sales.

Managing service companies

The traditional paradigm for organizations is often shown as a pyramid with the CEO placed at the apex, and separated by layers of managers from contact staff. This structure is hierarchical and has the effect of separating managers from clients. It has been remarked that the offices of middle managers may become the meeting ground for customer complaints and the directives of top managers, making it risky for the managers to resolve complaints in some circumstances (Noe, 1999). Peters and Austin (1985) have criticized the ability of managers in such organizations to take good decisions, and recommended 'turning the organizational pyramid upside down'. As shown in Figure 8.1, the result is a change in strategic thinking according to the principles of service management, with a change in priorities, and the responsibility for operational decisions moved from staff functions and management to those involved in the buyer and seller interactions and thus immediately responsible for the moments of truth which customers experience.

Zemke and Schaaf (1989) place customers in the centre of a triangle whose base is the system and the people involved in it, while the organization's service strategy forms the apex. Figure 8.2 implies that the function of management is to ensure effective service to its clients through resourcing the delivery system and supporting contact staff. Many managers are evidently uncomfortable with this approach to organizational structure, but it has been shown to be very effective for service companies.

Bethune (1998, at Continental Airlines) and Carlzon (1987, at SAS) are among a few CEOs who have written in detail, and passionately, about their experiences of turning around poorly performing airlines. DeFranco and Mok (2002) have described the improvement processes at Continental. Laszlo (1999) has analysed

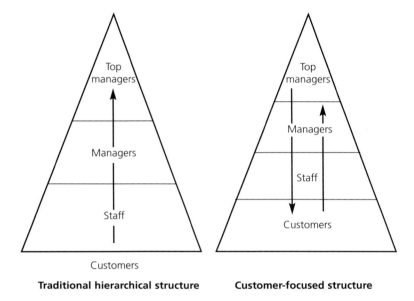

Figure 8.1 *Concepts of service organizations*

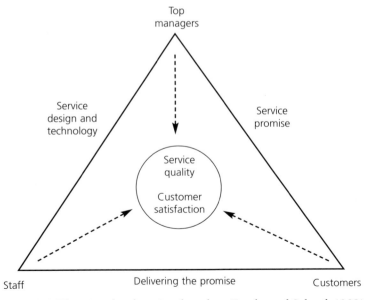

Figure 8.2 *The triangle of service (based on Zemke and Schaaf, 1989)*

how Southwest Airlines built operational and administrative excellence on a foundation of management commitment, customer focus, and employee involvement, and were awarded a Canada Award for Excellence. At Southwest Airlines the focus is on human interactions, and technology is thought of as providing the tools for those interactions. Laszlo states that legendary customer service comes from the heart not from cumbersome systems. As part of the efforts to keep simplifying administration and operation, meetings and reports are regularly reviewed to ensure that they serve an ongoing need. The operating philosophy at Southwest Airlines is to 'make an everyday reality their credo that customers come second to employees and still get great service' (ibid.: 90). Legendary customer service requires passion that transcends techniques and procedures: since commitment to service is a personal value, it must come from the heart.

The foregoing discussion reinforces the point of view put forward in this book. Two primary functions can be identified for service sector managers. One is fundamentally concerned with designing and resourcing an appropriate delivery system which also defines the parameters for service encounters between staff and customers. The second function is concerned with staff selection and training, and beyond that, the development of an organizational culture which empowers staff to solve problems on behalf of customers, within the company's cost or profit policies, and rewards them for contributing to customer satisfaction. The first management function – service design – underpins successful service delivery; if successful, it minimizes dysfunction and optimizes the second managerial objective – effective service transactions – thus maximizing the likelihood of providing satisfying experiences for customers.

Organizational climate

Shostack (1985: 244) has shown that in the best service firms

> a consistent pattern to the managerial process is evidenced. One sees a pronounced emphasis on controllable details, continuous investment in training, a concern with the customer's view and reward systems that place value on service quality. In poor service firms, however, one sees an internal rather than external orientation, a production orientation, a view of the customer as a transactions generator, a lack of attention to details affecting the customer, and a low priority placed on 'soft' service quality values.

There are many organizations in tourism, particularly certain hotels and restaurants, whose names are familiar icons of service excellence: their service strengths provide an excellent basis from which to gain the advantages of branding. Other businesses, including some major airlines, have been able to achieve success across a range of measures starting from the catalyst of a crisis, usually related to a significant change in their operating environments brought about by deregulation or by privatization. Laws (1991) has reported on the management turnaround at British Airways in the mid-1980s, a summary of which is given in Case study 8.1. Although dated, the case study illustrates the range of issues which companies in this type of predicament need to address. This has to be done in the context of a trading organization, so it requires sensitivity as well as strength. The case outlines a variety of methods adopted by Sir Colin Marshall, one of tourism's most respected service-oriented managers.

CASE STUDY 8.1

Changing the management style at British Airways

In the early 1980s British Airways (BA) was facing a crisis, and had been described as offering 'a "peasant class" of travel' (Campbell-Smith, 1986). Many of its international routes were losing money. The pressure of increasing competition, resulting in part from deregulation, together with increases in industrial disputes undermined the company's competitive position and many of its potential passengers opted for alternative carriers' services.

Colin (now Sir Colin) Marshall was appointed as Chief Executive. Sir Colin came to BA convinced that success in service industries depends on putting people first. His previous success at Avis had been widely recognized among service managers. The Avis slogan and operating code was 'Trying Harder'. Clients had been invited to phone named managers in the event that everything was not perfect. All Avis managers were expected to work at the counter to remain in contact with their customers.

Sir Colin established a steering group to look at ways of improving the level and consistency of customer service which BA offered. The framework for the steering group was set by BA's expressed aim of becoming the best airline in the world. Customer service was identified as the key corporate value, and meeting customer needs was the key area requiring radical change. Two decisions were taken which shaped the subsequent development of BA:

1. A Marketing Policy Group was established. This became known as the 'Gang of Four', and was also charged with the reorganization of BA. An external consultant advised on the reorganization, and other BA managers were coopted to the Group.
2. A presentation on 'Putting People First' which was accepted by Sir Colin Marshall led to a series of courses implemented throughout the company.

A new organization structure was announced in two White Books which remain confidential. Volume One set out the job specifications for senior positions which those selected were all asked to accept on one day, not then knowing who occupied other positions on the new organizational chart. Volume Two set out the company's philosophy for each division. On that single day (11 July 1983) 60 of the then 100 top managers left the company, and some managers were brought into the airline to fill high impact jobs. The new management team had an average age of 41, in contrast to the average of 20 years in management positions typical under the previous regime. The internal managers who survived were those who displayed entrepreneurial abilities and were prepared to take risks: these were characteristics which the old management had not rewarded.

In order to achieve an improved responsiveness towards their customers, a cultural revolution had to be carried out in a mature and functioning company. The objective was achieved through a series of staff and management development programmes.

1. Staff training starting from the bottom up

In the old days airline managers had concentrated on the backwheel of the corporate bicycle; they had invested in the power end of the business and training had concentrated on product knowledge. Now the interest focused on the front wheel. This did not drive the cyclist forward, but the skill of avoiding obstacles by precise steering was as important as pedalling powerfully. . . . it was not good business for a transport company to run into its passengers. (Farnham, 1986)

A company-wide rolling programme of training towards customer awareness was introduced. The programme was developed by Time Management International, an earlier version having proved successful for SAS, the Scandinavian airline. Starting in December 1983, all 37,000 BA staff went on the 'Putting People First' course, the first stage of the programme to orient staff towards a customer perspective.

- Putting People First (Phase 1). PPF (1) was a two-day event presented to about 150 people at each session, drawn from a range of customer-contact positions. Over a two-year period all employees were covered, not just the contact staff who were its original targets. Its central focus was the basic personal feelings of staff during their encounter with passengers, and ways of coping with stress.
- Customer First Teams. Volunteers formed quality circles to identify ways to improve the customer service experiences in their area of work. The positive outcomes were twofold:
  1. Staff offered significant suggestions for work improvements based on their experience.
  2. People felt they had gained some measure of control over the service they deliver.
- Customer First Training Review. The implications of developing contact staff sensitivities to customer service was that it became necessary to review all the existing training programmes.
- Putting People First (Phase 2). A one-day training event, similar to PPF (1), but intended for functional staff who did not deal directly with passengers. Its purpose was to demonstrate the importance of effective customer contact.
- A Day In The Life Of . . . PPF (3) took the form of 'an internal exhibition', a participative programme in which each

department showed the rest of the company what it does. This followed a desire expressed by people taking the earlier courses to find out more about what other departments did. In a Press Release BA summed up the purpose behind this major investment in training: 'The philosophy is that staff who have a greater awareness and understanding of the business should be able to provide high, professional standards of customer service, and also be in a strong position to act as ambassadors for the airline. Messages delivered at PPF courses are reinforced and the concept of teamwork at BA is encouraged.'

2. **Management changes and training**
A three-phase Managing People First programme was devised for BA's management.

- *Research among managers.* A study was commissioned to discover what senior managers considered to be important in their role, and what the shortcomings were. It identified five common aspects, shown in Table 8.1:

Table 8.1 *Key aspects of managerial roles*

---

(1) Trust
(2) Teamwork
(3) Taking responsibility
(4) Clarity of vision
(5) Motivation

A five-day residential programme was devised which centred on the right things for managers to do, rather than the operational methods involved.

- *Training.* A series of courses were concerned with the implementation of the appropriate management style.
- *Performance-related pay.* Management remuneration was based on regular appraisals against pre-agreed criteria. This generated an appraised–appraiser report which, together

with company reports, provided the basis of calculation for individual annual financial bonuses.

Marketing research

Underlying the changed philosophy of the company was a programme of market research. This formed the starting point for a fully integrated campaign to improve standards of service. The researchers were concerned with the views of both customers and staff, and they focused on where customers' goodwill, and hence their business, could be generated.

The research was conducted among air travellers, including BA and other airline passengers, to identify BA's image. BA had emerged as aloof, detached, not caring, not friendly, but technically competent, showing British cool and ability to cope with crises.

The second phase was an internal research project using repertory grid techniques on customer-contact staff to find out their views of customers. The major result of this survey was to identify a strong tendency to jump very quickly to stereotypes and then to deal with the stereotype and not the individual.

A 'Customer Service Department' was established to monitor market research and analyse staff and customer views. This department grew in significance and helped to produce Customer Service Standards and a Service Quality Audit. By 1990 it had become one of the seven major departments in the marketing section of the company, with line responsibility for all customer-contact staff (excluding cabin crew).

Based on Laws (1991)

Service design and organizational cultures

Studies of turnaround situations highlight the need for effective organizational climates embracing the new service paradigm. Zemke and Schaaf (1989) examined 101 companies providing excellent service and concluded that successful service firms share several features, summarized in Table 8.2. The philosophy of their study is about the use of external comparisons by which a company can evaluate the effectiveness of its own processes.

The use of benchmarking to identify industry best practice as a foundation to imitate or improve on existing services has become a recognized management tool and is also effective within organizational change processes (Chen, 1998; Pyo, 2002). Hines, Rich and Esain (1999) describe the value stream mapping approach in which benchmarking is concerned not with external comparisons but with how good a process could be.

Table 8.2 *Excellent service management*

- Managers are obsessive about listening to and responding to changing customer wants, needs and expectations
- They create and communicate a well-defined, customer-inspired service strategy
- They develop and maintain customer-friendly service delivery systems
- They hire, inspire and develop customer-oriented frontline people

---

Source: Zemke and Schaaf (1989)

A consistent theme in all of these studies is the crucial role of a company's CEO in transforming the culture of the organization towards customer service. Table 8.3 summarizes a range of authors' views on how this can be achieved.

Table 8.3 *Role of the CEO in implementing customer orientation*

The successful CEO:
(1) develops a compelling vision of the future
(2) translates the vision into reality by concentrating on keys to success
(3) is involved in the actions necessary to carry out the vision
(4) motivates employees to embrace the vision
(5) constantly articulates the vision throughout all organizational levels

---

Sources: Bennis (1968); Kanter (1983); Levinson (1971); Zaleznik (1977)

George and Gibson (1988: 13) have pointed out that techniques such as blueprinting a service 'can have the effect of changing forever the way people in organizations think about their operations. The blueprint facilitates a system-wide perspective of the entire service process allowing greater understanding of institutional quality.'

The design of the service, and its resourcing, are managerial responsibilities carried out away from immediate contact with clients, before the service is offered in the marketplace. Once an organization has begun to serve clients, the immediate pressures of customer contact take precedence, and the job becomes more urgent: it is about satisfying each client in ways which are meaningful to the individual. The lines of reporting and responsibility shift. The organization revolves around servicing the client, identifying his or her individual needs and endeavouring to satisfy these, within operational parameters. Traditional, top-down and directive management styles can be perceived by staff as barriers in this context, because jobs are often specified in resource- or role-specific terms rather than as the broad concept of striving to satisfy customers. Fundamentally, good service depends on an appropriate organizational culture which supports employees who are committed to quality in their own work.

The concept of organizational culture has been defined as

the pattern of shared values and beliefs that help individuals understand organizational functioning and thus provide them norms for behaviour in the organization. That is, organizational culture is related to the causality that members impute to organizational functioning. (Deshpande and Webster, 1989: 12)

Table 8.4 provides an overview of the factors in corporate culture management.

Table 8.4 *Corporate culture*

---

(1) *An appealing company philosophy ties employees emotionally to the company*
  • It ties employees to behaviour which is consistent with the philosophy
(2) *Creating an exchange of rights between employee and company*
  • The customer as a person with individual character
  • Being close to the customer speeds change
(3) *Regulating employee behaviour through culture rather than rules*
  • Managers as role models for employees
  • Employees as professionals
(4) *Culture heads everyone in the same direction*
  • Establishing principles to which all employees adhere
  • Pride in the company and its products
  • Institutionalized concern for product quality
  • Individual commitment to improving performance
  • Relationships with colleagues, suppliers, clients
  • Conception and execution of products to meet buyer expectations

---

Based on Horovitz and Panak (1992)

Interdependency in the holiday industry

From a managerial perspective, it is highly significant that tourists are likely to be served by some staff from other companies at certain stages in their holiday. Therefore, to ensure the overall quality of the holiday, managers need to coordinate their approaches to service delivery as they are mutually dependent. The dependency of one company on the performance of others has been discussed in the following terms:

> A company can be viewed as a node in an ever-widening pattern of interactions, in some of which it is a direct participant, some of which affect it indirectly and some of which occur independently of it. This web of interactions is so complex and multifarious as to deny full description or analysis. (Ford, Hakansson and Johansson, 1986: 35)

Upah and Fulton (1985) have also referred to this. 'Some customer contact tasks are performed more efficiently by intermediaries – usually relating to initial contact prior to delivery of the core service. . . . It weakens the control of the firm but may reduce costs.'

Relationship marketing is not concerned only with a firm's customer interfaces. It has a second meaning applied by the Nordic school to the networks within which organizations create and distribute their services. In a previous publication I defined the channels of distribution in tourism in the following way:

> An airline's distribution network consists of travel retailers selling to clients, tour operators who purchase blocks of seats, and its supplier network consists of complex sets of specialists at each airport it serves. These include check in agents, caterers, baggage handlers and the technical engineering and flight preparation services. Different organizations provide each of these at airports remote from the airline's home base. In fact, its destination based competitors often perform the role of suppliers, the airline reciprocating the arrangement at its base airport. Viewed in this way, the traditional perceptions of firms as competitors in a defined market place is only a partial analysis. In many instances, the management challenge and priority is to establish and maintain cooperative relationships with other organizations. (Laws, 2001a: 54)

The complex and interdependent nature of tourism has been noted at the scale of destinations by Buhalis (2000: 97) who remarked that 'destinations are an amalgam of tourism products, offering an integrated experience to consumers'.

Distribution management implies a long-term business relationship between members, but like other forms of human relationship it may be based on dislike and distrust or the recognition and nurturing of mutual advantages. The network of relationships between companies which underpins the tourism system, and the various ways in which this is organized, differs between different sectors and countries. Insights into the complexity and the dynamics of these relationships can be obtained by adopting the theoretical perspectives of network and alliance theory or relationship marketing (Gummesson, 1995; McKenna, 1994), and by viewing the holiday industry systemically.

> Relationship marketing strategies are concerned with a broader scope of external 'market' relationships which include suppliers, business referral and 'influence sources'. It also focuses on the staff relationships critical to the success of marketing plans and a resolution of the competing interests of customers, staff and shareholders by changing the way managers 'manage' the activities of the business. (Payne and Ballantyne, 1991: viii)

Gummesson has pointed out that even the most powerful companies such as IBM cannot develop, manufacture and market their products and services on their own. They enter into alliances with customers, competitors and suppliers to gain operational and cost advantages and for access to markets. He contrasted this perspective on management philosophies with the more familiar idea of competition. Whereas competition means winning someone over, or even destroying them to become the biggest in the field, this short-term, greedy way of doing business may prejudice long-term survival. The basis for cooperative networks in the tourism industry is summarized in Table 8.5.

Table 8.5 *Interdependencies in the tourism industry*

System member	Destination	Tour operator	Principals	Travel agent
Destination		Tour operator provides regular batches of visitors.	Quality of visitors' experiences depends on standards of hotels etc.	Staff knowledge and enthusiasm about a destination can be a critical factor in clients' choice.
Tour operator	Depends on primary features (climate, scenery, culture, ski infrastructure). Ability to exploit these commercially depends on the range and quality of tourism services offered.		Major expense for tour operator, also critical in ensuring customer expectations met.	Sales agent directing high street clients to specific tour operators' products.
Principals (hotels and airlines)	Depend on destinations for primary appeals and for social or technical infrastructure, such as sewers, roads, educational standards of staff and airport facilities.	Tour operators provide flows of customers throughout season to specific destinations at agreed prices.		Generally minimal for holiday products as their services are embodied in tour operators' products.

Table 8.5 *continued*

System member	Destination	Tour operator	Principals	Travel agent
Travel agent	Depends on destinations for briefings, staff familiarization tours and point-of-sale materials.	Dependent on tour operators for creating a market through advertising, for staff training, brochures, and CRS for sales.	Depends on hotels and airlines for sales support and staff training.	

Source: Laws (1997a)

This led Gummesson (1999) to postulate an imaginary organization, in which many of the resources, processes and staff are outside the main organization's legal and accounting boundaries. Such networks depend on a leader company and a shared business mission. Similarly, Handy (1990: 12) discussed a federative organization: 'All the suggested organizational formats are challenging the functional hierarchy and replacing it with more functional and process oriented approaches.' These and other authors recognize the simultaneous existence of competition and collaboration within regulatory and institutional frameworks.

The limits of management control

Service delivery systems: the customer interfaces

The purpose of designing and managing service systems is to enable the organization to deliver appropriate, satisfying services to the clients it serves, and to do this in ways which satisfy organizational objectives, whether these be profit, growth, efficiency or excellence. So the organization's resources, including the skills and professionalism of its managers and staff, should be focused on customer needs and presented in ways which customers can enjoy.

Many services take place over extended periods – a couple of hours for a restaurant meal, a day and a night for a hotel stay, a week or a month for a holiday. This presents the customer with multiple points and types of interaction, the moments of truth in which he or she tests and evaluates service quality. The importance of contact with the organization's equipment and staff, and with those of service partners has been noted. Customers also notice and respond to the service setting: the ambience of the restaurant interior, even its accessibility in good weather or inclement, are factored into their evaluation of the total service quality. So is the behaviour of other clients, as this too can impact on service experiences, adding to one client's pleasure, or detracting from his or her own enjoyment.

Some of the factors which influence customer satisfaction are not usually regarded as part of a manager's responsibility, for example he cannot be expected to intervene unless other clients become unruly, and there is little that can be done in the short term to alter the ambience or setting of a service. However, most of its features are controllable, and prior planning can help create situations which are more (or less) likely to result in client satisfaction.

> Most of a company's marketing is not carried out by the professional full time marketer, but by the amateur part time marketer (PTM), who is omnipotent both inside and outside a company. The PTM influences customer relations and revenue without belonging to the marketing or sales department. (Gummesson, 1991: 60)

This places the responsibility for the firm's success back with managers, because as Berry (1995: 140) has stated: 'dependability and accuracy can be designed into a service system, or designed out of it . . . [The real culprit for service mistakes] is often . . . a needlessly complicated and failure prone service system.' As has been shown in previous chapters, analysis of customer correspondence indicates that people do not experience a service which had essentially similar characteristics for each of them in the same way. An explanation for this phenomenon is that each person interprets selected aspects of the tourism service in his or her own terms and thus may find the experience more (or less) satisfying than other passengers. The significance of this lies in the limitations it implies for universal quality standards and control systems in tourism. Indeed, this line of study strongly suggests that the criteria of tourism quality are determined by three sets of people: the client and contact staff as well as management. The quality of any tourism service is therefore a complex concept defined in the interaction between producer and client. Effective management of tourism quality therefore depends on a close match between the intentions and actions of the service provider and the expectations of clients.

The complexity of service industry transactions has been a major focus of this book. Many factors impinge on customer satisfaction. Noe (1999) noted that attributes such as the weather or insects are not really under the direct control of National Park managers, but they may trigger strong emotional responses among guests adversely affected by them. Table 8.6 lists a number of factors under the control of managers, and others which they cannot normally control.

Table 8.6 *Management control of factors affecting customer satsfaction*

Factors managers can control:
 (1) Access
 (2) Communications
 (3) Competence
 (4) Courtesy
 (5) Credibility
 (6) Reliability
 (7) Responsiveness
 (8) Security
 (9) Tangibles
(10) Understanding the customer

Factors managers have little control over:
 (1) The customer's attitude, influenced by word of mouth recommendation
 (2) The customer's personal needs
 (3) Any past experience the customer may have had with that company

---

Based on Zeithmal, Berry and Parasuraman (1988)

Further considerations

The scope of this book is necessarily limited by its size, and a number of important topics have been given little attention, while others have not been addressed at all. Tourism is a global industry in that any company, destination, attraction or property is likely to entertain clients from several countries at any one time, and furthermore many are staffed by people from a variety of cultural backgrounds. This raises the issues of cultural differences in service expectations. A study by Mok and Armstrong (1996) applied SERVQUAL expectations instruments to hotel guests' service expectations and found that some dimensions are significant to guests no matter what their country of origin, while other factors appear to differ between cultures. Winsted (1997) found that American and Japanese consumers' views of service encounters differ. Kim, Pan and Park (1998) also noted significant differences between Chinese, Korean and American consumers. Lee and Ulgado (1997: 39) commented:

> Understanding of customer perceptions of service quality and value is particularly important to international service firms because such perceptions are susceptible to cultural differences. In countries with different cultures, tastes and living habits, US service companies need to be aware and adaptive to local needs . . . . Hence, the cultural distance between the US and the foreign host country would be a major concern for foreign investment of US service firms.

This is a developing area of research in tourism. Research focused on the experiences of visitors from different cultures includes Reisenger and Waryszak (1994); Rao and Hashimoto (1997); Ford, Joseph and Joseph (1999); and Crotts and Erdmann (2000).

Other topics which I have mentioned in this book and which require more attention from other authors include the rapidly developing use of information technology to disseminate information about services, and particularly its roles in influencing the formation of service quality expectations at the purchasing stage. Two further aspects of tourist service systems must be noted. These are the impacts of the industry on the staff who depend on it for their livelihoods, and its impacts on the residents in destination areas.

Conclusion

The main arguments put forward in this book are summarized in the appendix in the form of a brief slide presentation, following a style introduced by Gianna Moscardo (1999).

The fundamental quality issue for tourism and hospitality organizations is that holidays are expensive discretionary purchases. Unless the forms of tourism which destinations and operators offer to the public are enticing and the experiences of journeys, hotels, destination places, people and activities satisfy tourists, the industry has little prospect of sustaining itself in the future.

The final word in shaping the future of the tourism industry lies with tourists, who express their views through selecting operators (and destinations) which provide the type of experiences they seek, or by not returning to those which they have disliked. Tourism and hospitality researchers can contribute to the better management of the industry, locally and globally, by more rigorous research into quality in tourism as a basis for future improvements in these industries' management, marketing and development.

Appendix:
Slides for a management
development workshop

Slide 1

Service quality: what to measure

- To be effective in managing the quality of any service, managers and researchers need to be sure that what they are monitoring is relevant

- Both technical- and customer-oriented perspectives on quality are important for marketplace success

- A clear understanding of the ways in which they are relevant to a particular service requires research, and managerial insights

Slide 2

Service quality: ownership, participation and control

- Effective service management requires specialized approaches
  - service transactions involve the interactions of people: staff and client
  - subcontracting organizations also have direct contact with clients
- The vision of an organization inspires its ability to present its service with a style which clearly distinguishes it from its competitors
- This leads to the need for consistent quality
- Competition leads to the need for constant improvements to service delivery

Slide 3

Service delivery systems: design approaches

- Services can be designed
- Blueprinting is a way of mapping an existing service
- The technique helps organizations gain a customer perspective on their service
- Blueprinting can identify potential problems in the delivery system

Slide 4

Service delivery systems: performance mapping methods

- The designed service can be specified in terms of performance criteria for each element
- Customers' views of the service can be mapped on to service blueprints to prioritize those aspects of the service requiring attention

Slide 5

Service delivery systems:
the customer interfaces

- The organization's resources, including the skills and professionalism of its managers and staff, should be focused on customer needs, and presented in ways which customers enjoy

- Many services take place over extended periods; this presents the customer with many moments of truth in which he or she tests and evaluates service quality

Slide 6

Service delivery systems:
organizational cultures

- The design of the service, and resourcing decisions, are managerial responsibilities best carried out before the service is offered to the public

- The lines of reporting and responsibility shift during service performance as the organization focuses on servicing the client, identifying his or her individual needs and endeavouring to satisfy these, within operational parameters

Slide 7

Service quality: getting it right

- Disgruntled clients become so, and adversely affect fellow clients, usually because some aspect of the service has failed, in their opinion
- In most cases, a service problem is not immediately a service crisis, although it may escalate into one
- There are three phases to dealing with service problems
  - the immediate challenge is to recognize that a problem has occurred
  - the response should be to remedy the defect promptly
  - the organization can learn from the customer's experience

Slide 8

Tourism and hospitality service quality: getting it even better

	People	Technical processes	Business partners
Tactical measures			
Responsiveness	✔		✔
Refinement		✔	
Strategic measures			
Research	✔	✔	✔
Redesign		✔	
Redefine relationships and responsibilities	✔		✔

Bibliography

Ableson, R. P. (1976) 'Script processing in attitude formation and decision making', in J. S. Corroll and J. W. Payne (eds) *Cognition and Social Behaviour*. Hillside, NJ: Erlbaum.

Adams, J. S. (1976) 'The structure and dynamics of behavior in organizational boundary roles', in M. D. Dunette (ed.) *Handbook of Industrial and Organizational Psychology*. Chicago, IL: Rand McNally.

Ahmad, S. (2002) 'Service failures and customer defection: a closer look at online shopping experiences'. *Managing Service Quality*, **12**(1), 19–29.

Akehurst, G. (1996) 'Market structure, behaviour and performance in consumer service industries'. PhD Thesis, Nottingham Trent University.

Albrecht, K. and Zemke, R. (1985) *Service America*. Homewood, IL: Dow Jones-Irwin.

Allwein, G. (ed.) (1996) *Logic Reasoning with Diagrams*. Oxford: Oxford University Press.

Anderson, E. W., Fornell, C. and Lehmann, D. R. (1994) 'Customer satisfaction and word of mouth'. *Journal of Service Marketing*, **1**(1), 5–17.

Argenti, J. (1997) 'Stakeholders: the case against'. *Long Range Planning*, **30**(3), 442–5.

Asseal, H. (1987) *Consumer Behavior and Marketing Action*. Boston, MA: Kent Publication Co.

Avila, J. and Setter, R. (1980) *Traffic Flow Model*. Burbank, CA: Lockheed.

Band, W. (1991) *Creating Value for Customers: Designing and Implementing a Total Corporate Strategy*. New York: Wiley.

Barclay, I., Holroyd, P. and Poolton, J. (1994) 'Management and innovation in a complex environment'. *Leadership and Organizational Development Journal*, **15**(7), 33–44.

Bateson, J. (1977) 'Do we need service marketing?'. *Marketing Consumer Services: New Insights Report*, Boston, MA: Marketing Science Institute, 75–115.

Bateson, J. (2002) 'Consumer performance and quality in services'. *Managing Service Quality*, **12**(4), 206–9.

Baum, T. (1998) 'Mature doctoral candidates: the case in hospitality education'. *Tourism Management*, **19**(5), 463–74.

Bejou, D. and Palmer, A. (1998) 'Service failure and loyalty: an exploratory empirical study of airline customers'. *Journal of Services Marketing*, **12**(1), 7–22.

Bennet, R. C. (1991) 'The marketing of tourist destinations: why customer service is so important'. Working paper received from author.

Bennis, W. (1968) *Temporary Society*. New York: Harper and Row.

Berger, P. D. and Nasr, N. I. (1998) 'Customer lifetime value: marketing models and applications'. *Journal of Interactive Marketing*, **12**(1), 17–30.

Berkely, B. (1996) 'Analysing service blueprints using phase distribution'. *European Journal of Operational Research*, **88**(1), 152–64.

Berno, T. and Bricken, K. (2001) 'Sustainable tourism development: the long road from theory to practice'. *International Journal of Economic Development*, **3**(3), 1–18.

Berry, L. (1995) *On Great Service: A Framework For Action*. New York: The Free Press.

Bertalanffy, L. (1968) *General Systems Theory*. New York: Brazillier.

Bethune, G. (1998) *From Worst to First: Behind the Scenes of Continental's Remarkable Comeback*. New York: Wiley.

Bettencourt, L. (1997) 'Customer voluntary performance: customers as partners in service delivery'. *Journal of Retailing*, **73**(3), 383–406.

Bitner, M. (1992) 'Servicescapes: the impact of physical surroundings on customers and employees'. *Journal of Marketing*, **56**, April, 57–71.

Bitner, M. J., Booms, B. H. and Mohr, L. (1994) 'Critical service encounters: the employee's point of view'. *Journal of Marketing*, **58**(4), 95–106.

Bitner, M. J., Booms, B. H. and Tetreault, M. S. (1990) 'The service encounter: diagnosing favorable and unfavorable incidents'. *Journal of Marketing*, **54**, January, 71–84.

Blackman, B. A. (1985) 'Making a service more tangible can make it more manageable', in J. A. Czepiel, M. R. Solomon and C. F. Surprenant (eds) *The Service Encounter: Managing Employee/Customer Interaction In Service Business*. Lexington, MA: Lexington Books, 291–302.

Block, P. (1995) 'Seeking the ideal form: product design and consumer response'. *Journal of Marketing*, **59**, 16–29.

Bloemer, J., de Ruyter, K. and Wetzels, M. (1999) 'Linking perceived service quality and service loyalty: a multi-dimensional perspective'. *Journal of Marketing*, **33**, 1082–106.

Bonoma, T. (1985) 'Case research in marketing: opportunities, problems and a process'. *Journal of Marketing Research*, **22**, May, 199–208.

Booms, B. H. and Bitner, M. J. (1981) 'Marketing strategies and organization structures for service firms', in J. Donnelley and W. George (eds) *Marketing of Services*. Chicago, IL: AMA, 51–67.

Botschen, G., Bstieler, L. and Woodside, A. (1996) 'Sequence-oriented problem identification within service encounters'. *Journal of Euromarketing*, **5**(2), 19–52.

Boulding, W., Kalra, A., Staelin, R. and Zeithmal, V. A. (1993) 'A dynamic process model of service quality: from expectations to behavioral intentions'. *Journal of Marketing Research*, **30**, 7–27.

Bowen, D. E. and Schneider, B. (1985) 'Boundary spanning role employees and the service encounter: some guidelines for management and research', in J. A. Czepiel, M. R. Solomon and C. F. Surprenant (eds) *The Service Encounter: Managing Employee/Customer Interaction In Service Business*. Lexington, MA: Lexington Books, 125–48.

Brady, M. K. and Robertson, C. J. (2001) 'Searching for a consensus on the antecedent role of service quality and satisfaction: an exploratory cross-national study'. *Journal of Business Research*, **51**(1), 53–60.

Britt, S. H. (1975) 'How Weber's Law can be applied to marketing'. *Business Horizons*, February, 21.

Brown, S. L. and Eisenhardt, K. M. (1995) 'Product development: past research, present findings, and future directions'. *Academy of Management Review*, **20**(2), 343–78.

Brown, S. W., Cowles, D. L. and Tuten, T. L. (1996) 'Service recovery: its value and limitations as a retail strategy'. *International Journal of Service Industry Management*, **7**(5), 32–46.

Brown, T., Churchill, G. and Peter, J. (1993) 'Improving the measurement of service quality'. *Journal of Retailing*, **69**(1), 127–39.

Buhalis, D. (2000) 'Marketing the competitive destination of the future'. *Tourism Management*, **21**(1), 97–116.

Buhalis, D. and Laws, E. (eds) (2001) *Tourism Distribution Channels: Practices, Issues and Transformations*. London: Continuum.

Bull, A. (1991) *The Economics of Travel and Tourism*. New York: Wiley.

Buttle, F. (1995) 'SERVQUAL: review, critique, research agenda'. *European Journal of Marketing*, **30**, 8–32.

Buzzell, R. D. and Gale, B. T. (1987) *The PIMS Principles*. New York: The Free Press.

Callan, R. J. (1998) 'The critical incident technique in hospitality research: an illustration from the UK lodge sector'. *Tourism Management*, **19**(1), 93–8.

Campbell, C. (1987) *The Romantic Ethic and the Spirit of Modern Consumerism*. Oxford: Basil Blackwell.

Campbell-Smith, D. (1986) *Struggle for Take-Off: The British Airways Story*. London: Hodder and Stoughton.

Carlzon, J. (1987) *Moments of Truth*. New York: Harper and Row.

Carmen, J. M. (1990) 'Consumer perceptions of service quality: an assessment of the SERVQUAL dimensions'. *Journal of Retailing*, **66**(1), 33–55.

Carney, T. F. (1972) *Content Analysis: A Technique for Systematic Inference from Communications*. London: Batsford.

Casson, L. (1994) *Travel In The Ancient World*. Baltimore, MD: The Johns Hopkins University Press.

Chadee, D. and Mattsson, J. (1996) 'An empirical assessment of customer satisfaction in tourism'. *Service Industries Journal*, **16**(3), 305–20.

Chase, R. B. (1978) 'Where does the customer fit in a service organization?' *Harvard Business Review*, November–December, 137–42.

Chase, R. B. and Tansik, D. A. (1983) 'The customer contact model for organizational design'. *Management Science*, **49**, 1037–50.

Checkland, P. and Scholes, J. (1990) *Soft Systems Methodology in Action*. Chichester: Wiley.

Chen, W. (1998) 'Benchmarking quality goals in service systems'. *Journal of Services Marketing*, **12**(2), 113–28.

Chenet, P., Tynan, C. and Money, A. (1999) 'Service performance gap: re-evaluation and redevelopment'. *Journal of Business Research*, **46**, 133–47.

Chisnall, P. M. (1985) *Marketing: A Behavioural Analysis*. London: McGraw-Hill.

Clow, K., Kurz, D., Ozment, J. and Beng Soo Ong (1997) 'The antecedents of consumer expectations of services: an empirical study across four industries'. *The Journal of Services Marketing*, **11**(4), 230–48.

Cooney, M. (1995) 'Airtours plots a course for a growing market'. *Travel Weekly*, March, 6.

Cowell, D. W. (1986) *The Marketing of Services*. London: Heinemann.

Craig, M. (2000) *Thinking Visually: Business Applications of Core Diagrams*. London: Continuum.

Crawford, M. (1997) *New Product Management*. Chicago, IL: Irwin.

Cronin, J. and Taylor, S. (1992) 'Measuring service quality: a re-examination and extension'. *Journal of Marketing*, **56**, 55–68.

Crosby, P. (1984) *Quality Without Tears*. New York: New American Library.

Crotts, J. and Erdmann, R. (2000) 'Does national culture influence consumers' evaluation of travel services? A test of Hofstede's model of cross-cultural differences'. *Managing Service Quality*, **10**(6), 410–19.

Czepiel, J. A., Solomon, M. R. and Surprenant, C. F. (1985) (eds) *The Service Encounter: Managing Employee/Customer Interaction In Service Business*. Lexington, MA: Lexington Books.

Dale, B. G., Lascelles, D. M. and Lloyd, A. (1994) 'Supply chain management', in B. G. Dale (ed.) *Managing Quality*. Hemel Hempstead: Prentice Hall, 292–313.

Davidson, W. E., Sweeney, D. J. and Stampfl, R. W. (1988) *Retailing Management* (6th edition). New York: Wiley.

Davis, F. W. (1989) 'Enabling is as important as empowering: a case for extended service blueprinting', in *Service Excellence: Marketing's Impact on Performance*. AMA Conference Proceedings. Chicago, IL: AMA.

de Ruyter, K. and Wetzels, M. (2000) 'Customer equity considerations in service recovery: a cross-industry perspective'. *International Journal of Service Industry Management*, **11**(1), 91–108.

DeFranco, A. L. and Mok, C. (2002) 'Continental Airlines: turnaround through customer focused strategies', in E. Laws (ed.) *Tourism Marketing: Quality and Service Management Perspectives*. London: Continuum, 87–99.

Dellaert, B., Ettema, D. and Lindh, C. (1998) 'Multi-faceted tourist travel decisions: a constraint-based conceptual framework to describe tourists' sequential choices of travel components'. *Tourist Management*, **19**(4), 313–20.

Deming, W. E. (1982) *Quality, Productivity and Competitive Position*. Cambridge, MA: MIT Centre for Advanced Engineering Study.

Deshpande, R. (1983) 'Paradigm lost: on theory and method in research in marketing'. *Journal of Marketing*, **47**, Autumn, 101–10.

Deshpande, R. and Webster, F. E. (1989) 'Organizational culture and marketing: defining the research agenda'. *Journal of Marketing*, **53**, 3–15.

Dickey, J. D. (1998) 'Creating a customer satisfaction measurement system'. *Industrial Management*, **40**(2), 8–11.

Done, K. (2003) 'You cannot retire such an aircraft without a tear'. *Financial Times*, 11 April, 9.

Duadel, S. and Vialle, G. (1994) *Yield Management: Applications to Air Transport and Other Service Industries*. Paris: Institut du Transport Aerien.

Dwyer, L., Murray, P. and Mott, R. (1998) 'Continuous improvement in hospitality: a case study approach'. *Australian Journal of Hospitality Management*, **5**(1), 19–31.

Edgett, S. (1994) 'The traits of successful service development'. *Journal of Services Marketing*, **8**(3), 40–9.

Edvardsson, B., Hagland, L. and Mattsson, J. (1995) 'Analysis, planning, improvisation and control in the development of new services'. *International Journal of Service Industry Management*, **6**(2), 24–35.

Edvardsson, B. and Strandvik, T. (2000) 'Is a critical incident critical for a customer relationship?' *Managing Service Quality*, **10**(2), 82–91.

Eiglier, P. and Langeard, E. (1987) *Servuction*. Paris: McGraw-Hill.

Eisenhardt, K. (1989) 'Building theories from case study research'. *Academy of Management Review*, **14**(4), 532–50.

Ekinci, Y. and Riley, M. (1999) 'Measuring hotel quality: back to basics'. *International Journal of Hospitality Management*, **11**, 287–93.

Engel, J. F., Blackwell, R. D. and Miniard, P. W. (1986) *Consumer Behaviour*. New York: Dryden Press.

Eriksen, J. and Liu, E. (1979) *Effects of Fare and Travel Time on the Demand for Domestic Airtransportation*. Langley, VA: NASA (NASA 1-15268).

Estelami, H. (2000) 'Competitive and procedural determinants of delight and disappointment in consumer complaint outcomes'. *Journal of Service Research*, **2**(3), 285–300.

Evans, F. B. (1963) 'Selling as a dyadic relationship'. *American Behavioural Scientist*, May, 76–9.

Farnham, N. (1986) 'Education for airlines – proceedings or seminar', in E. Laws (ed.) *Transport Studies: What Role in a Tourism Course?* London: Tourism Society.

Faulkner, H. W. and Russell, R. (1997) 'Chaos and complexity in tourism: in search of a new perspective'. *Pacific Tourism Review*, **1**(2), 93–102.

Feigenbaum, A. (1956) 'Total quality control'. *Harvard Business Review*, November–December, 94–8.

Festinger, L. A. (1957) *A Theory of Cognitive Dissonance*. Palo Alto, CA: Stanford University Press.

Fick, G. and Ritchie, J. (1991) 'Measuring service quality'. *Journal of Travel Research*, **30**(2), 2–9.

Fisk, R., Brown, S. and Bitner, M. J. (1993) 'Tracking the evolution of services marketing literature'. *Journal of Retailing*, **69**(1), 61–91.

Flanagan, J. C. (1954) 'The critical incident technique'. *Psychological Bulletin*, **51**, 327–57.

Fodness, D. and Murray, B. (1997) 'Tourist information search'. *Annals of Tourism Research*, **24**(3), 503–23.

Fojt, M. (1996) 'Editorial'. *The International Journal of Bank Marketing*, **14**(5), 2.

Ford, D., Hakansson, H. and Johansson, J. (1986) 'How do companies interact?' *Industrial Marketing and Purchasing*, **1**(1), 34–48.

Ford, J., Joseph, M. and Joseph, B. (1999) 'Importance-performance analysis as a strategic tool for service marketers: the case of service quality perceptions of business students in New Zealand and the USA'. *Journal of Services Marketing*, **13**(2), 171–86.

Fornell, C. (1981) 'Increasing the organizational influence of corporate consumer affairs departments'. *Journal of Consumer Affairs*, **15**, Winter, 191–213.

Fornell, C. and Wernerfelt, B. (1987) 'Defensive marketing strategy by customer complaint management: a theoretical analysis'. *Journal of Marketing Research*, **XXIV**, November, 337–46.

Gardner, M. P. (1987) 'The effect of mood states on consumer information processing'. *Research in Consumer Behaviour*, **2**(1), 113–35.

Garvin, D. A. (1988) *Managing Quality: The Strategic and Competitive Edge*. New York: The Free Press.

George, W. R. and Gibson B. E. (1988) *Blueprinting: A Tool for Managing Quality in Organizations*. Sweden: QUIS Symposium at the University of Karlstad, August.

George, W. R. and Kelly, T. (1983) *Personal Selling of Services: Emerging Perspectives on Service Marketing*. Chicago, IL: AMA.

Gilbert, G. R. and Parhizgari, A. M. (2000) 'Organizational effectiveness indicators to support service quality'. *Managing Service Quality*, 10(1), 46–52.

Gleick, J. (1987) *Chaos*. London: Sphere Books.

Goffman, E. (1959) *The Presentation of Self in Everyday Life*. New York: Doubleday.

Grönroos, C. (1982) *Strategic Management and Marketing in the Service Sector*. London: Chartwell-Bratt.

Grönroos, C. (1990) *Service Management and Marketing: Managing the Moments of Truth In Service Competition*. Lexington, MA: Lexington Books.

Grönroos, C. (1998) 'Marketing services: a case of a missing product'. *Journal of Business and Industrial Marketing*, 13(3/4), 322–38.

Grönroos, C. (2001) 'The perceived service quality concept – a mistake?' *Managing Service Quality*, 11(3), 150–2.

Gummesson, E. (1988) 'Service quality and product quality combined'. *Review of Business*, 9(3), 1–11.

Gummesson, E. (1990) 'Service design'. *The Total Quality Magazine*, 2(2), 97–101.

Gummesson, E. (1991) *Qualitative Methods in Management Research*. London: Sage.

Gummesson, E. (1993) *Quality Management in Service Organizations*. Stockholm, Sweden: International Service Quality Association/CTF.

Gummesson, E. (1995) 'Making relationship marketing operational'. *International Journal of Service Industry Management*, 5(5), 5–20.

Gummesson, E. (1999) *Total Relationship Marketing: Rethinking Marketing Management from 4Ps to 30Rs*. Oxford: Butterworth-Heinemann.

Gutek, B. A., Cherry, B., Bhappu, A. D., Schneider, S. and Woolf, L. (2000) 'Features of service relationships and encounters'. *Work and Occupations*, 27(3), 319–52.

Handy, C. (1990) *The Age of Unreason*. Boston, MA: Harvard Business School Press.

Harari, O. (1999) 'The power of complaints'. *Management Review*, July–August, 31–4.

Harington, D. and Akehurst, G. (1996) 'An exploratory investigation into managerial perceptions of service quality in UK hotels'. *Progress in Tourism and Hospitality Research*, 2(2), 135–50.

Hauser J. R. and Clausing, D. (1988) 'The house of quality'. *Harvard Business Review*, May, 63–7.

Hayes, B. E. (1998) *Measuring Customer Satisfaction: Survey Design, Use, and Statistical Analysis Methods*. Milwaukee, WI: American Society for Quality.

Haywood, K. (1997) 'Revising and implementing the marketing concept as it applies to tourism'. *Tourism Management*, **11**(3), 195–205.

Heape, R. (1994) 'Outward bound'. *Tourism Society Journal*, **83**, 4–5.

Heskett, J. L., Jones, T. O., Loveman, G. W., Sasser, W. E. and Schlessinger, L. A. (1994) 'Putting the service profit chain to work'. *Harvard Business Review*, March–April, 164–74.

Hill, N. and Alexander, J. (2000) *Handbook of Customer Satisfaction and Loyalty Measurement* (2nd edition). Aldershot: Gower Publishing.

Hines, P., Rich, N. and Esain, A. (1999) 'Value stream mapping: a distribution industry application'. *Benchmarking: An International Journal*, **6**(1), 33–56.

Hirschman, E. C. (1986) 'Humanistic inquiry in marketing research: philosophy, method, and criteria'. *Journal of Marketing Research*, **23**, 237–49.

Hjalager, A. (2001) 'Quality in tourism through the empowerment of tourists'. *Managing Service Quality*, **11**(4), 287–96.

Hoch, S. J. and Deighton, J. (1989) 'Managing from what consumers learn from experience'. *Journal of Marketing*, **53**, April, 1–20.

Hollins, G. and Hollins, B. (1991) *Total Design: Managing the Design Process in the Service Sector*. London: Pitman.

Holloway, J. C. and Robinson, R. (1995) *Marketing for Tourism* (3rd edition). Harlow: Longman.

Horovitz, J. and Panak, M. J. (1992) *Total Customer Satisfaction: Lessons from 50 European Companies with Top Service*. London: Financial Times/Pitman.

Howard, J. A. (1977) *Consumer Behaviour: Applications of Theory*. New York: McGraw-Hill.

Hudson, S. and Shephard, G. (1998) 'Measuring service quality at tourist destinations: an application of importance-performance analysis to an alpine ski resort'. *Journal of Travel and Tourism Marketing*, **7**(3), 61–77.

Hughes, R. (1993) *Culture of Complaint*. New York: Warner books.

Hunt, H. K. (1977) *Conceptualization and Measurement of Consumer Satisfaction and Dissatisfaction*. Cambridge, MA: Marketing Science Institute.

Imrie, B. C., Cadogan, J. W. and McNaughton, R. (2002) 'The service quality construct on a global stage'. *Managing Service Quality*, **12**(1), 10–18.

Ingram, H. (2000) 'Using soft systems methodology to manage hotels: a case study'. *Managing Service Quality*, **10**(1), 6–10.

ISO 9004-2 (1990) *Quality Management and Quality Systems Elements. Part 2: Guidelines for Services*. Homebush, NSW: The Standards Association of Australia.

Johns, N. (1999) 'Quality management', in B. Brotherton (ed.) *The Handbook of Contemporary Hospitality Management Research*. Chichester: Wiley, 333–49.

Johns, N. and Clark, S. L. (1993) 'The quality audit: a means of monitoring the service provided by museums and galleries'. *Journal of Museum Managership and Curatorship*, **12**, 360–6.

Johnson, R., Tsiros, M. and Lancioni, R. (1995) 'Measuring service quality: a systems approach'. *Journal of Services Marketing*, **9**(5), 6–19.

Johnston, B. (1995) 'The determinants of service quality: satisfiers and dissatisfiers'. *International Journal of Service Industry Management*, **6**(5), 23–48.

Johnston, R. (1999) 'Service transaction analysis: assessing and improving the customer's experience'. *Managing Service Quality*, **9**(2), 102–9.

Jones, P., Lockwood, A. and Kirk, D. (2002) *Hospitality Operations: A Systems Based Approach*. London: Continuum.

Jorgensen, D. L. (1989) *Participant Observation: A Methodology for Human Studies*. London: Sage.

Josephides, N. (1994) 'More to it than meets the eye'. *Travel Weekly*, 14 September, 11.

Juran, J. M. (1982) *Upper Management and Quality*. New York: Juran Institute.

Kandampully, J. (2000) 'The impact of demand fluctuation on the quality of service: a tourism industry example'. *Managing Service Quality*, **10**(1), 10–19.

Kanter, R. (1983) *The Change Masters*. New York: Simon and Schuster.

Kaspar, C. (1989) 'Recent developments in tourism research and education at university level', in S. F. Witt and L. Moutinho (eds) *Tourism Marketing and Management Handbook*. London: Prentice Hall, 443–6.

Kast, F. E. and Rosenzweig, J. E. (1985) *Organization and Management: A Systems and Contingency Approach* (4th edition). New York: McGraw-Hill.

Katz, D. and Kahn, R. L. (1978) *The Social Psychology of Organizations*. New York: Wiley.

Keefe, R. and Smith, P. (1999) *Vagueness: A Reader*. Cambridge, MA: MIT Press.

Kim, D., Pan, Y. and Park, H. (1998) 'High- versus low-context culture: a comparison of Chinese, Korean, and American culture'. *Psychology & Marketing*, **15**(6), 507–21.

Kimes, S. E. (1994) 'Perceived fairness of yield management'. *Cornell H. R. A. Quarterly*, February, 22–9.

Kingman-Brundage, J. (1989) 'Blueprinting for the bottom line', in *Service Excellence: Marketing's Impact on Performance.* AMA Conference Proceedings. Chicago, IL: AMA.

Kirk, D. (1995) 'Hard and soft systems: a common paradigm for operations management?' *International Journal of Contemporary Hospitality Management,* 7(5), 13–16.

Kotler, P. (1998) *Marketing* (4th edition). New York/Sydney: Prentice Hall.

Kotler, P. and Armstrong, G. (1999) *Principles of Marketing* (International edition). London: Prentice Hall.

Krippendorf, J. (1987) *The Holiday Makers.* London: Heinemann.

Lalonde, B. J. and Zinzser, P. H. (1976) *Customer Service: Meaning and Measurement.* Chicago, IL: National Council of Physical Distribution Management.

Lashley, C. (1997) *Empowering Service Excellence: Beyond the Quick Fix.* London: Cassell.

Laszlo, G. P. (1999) 'Southwest Airlines – living total quality in a service organization'. *Managing Service Quality,* 9(2), 90–5.

Laws, E. (1986) 'Identifying and managing the consumerist gap'. *Service Industries Journal,* 6(2), 131–43.

Laws, E. (1991) *Tourism Marketing: Service and Quality Management Perspectives.* Cheltenham: Stanley Thornes.

Laws, E. (1992) 'Service analysis – a consumerist gap taxonomy'. *Service Industries Journal,* 12(1), 117–24.

Laws, E. (1995) *Tourist Destination Management: Issues, Analysis and Policies.* London: Routledge.

Laws, E. (1997) *Managing Packaged Tourism, Relationships, Responsibility and Service Quality in the Inclusive Holiday Industry.* London: Thomson International Business Press.

Laws, E. (1998) 'Conceptualising visitor satisfaction management in heritage settings: an exploratory blueprinting analysis of Leeds Castle, Kent'. *Tourism Management,* 19(6), 545–54.

Laws, E. (2001a) 'Two ways of serving pizza – a comparative study of high and low contact services using blueprint techniques', in A. Roper and Y. Guerier (eds) *A Decade of Hospitality Management Research.* Pontypool: CHME Threshold Press, 37–55.

Laws, E. (2001b) 'Distribution channel analysis for leisure travel', in D. Buhalis and E. Laws (eds) *Tourism Distribution Channels: Practices, Issues and Transformations.* London: Continuum, 53–72.

Laws, E. (ed.) (2002) *Tourism Marketing: Quality and Service Management Perspectives.* London: Continuum.

Laws, E. and Cooper, C. (1998) 'Inclusive Tours and commodification: the marketing constraints for mass market resorts'. *Journal of Vacation Marketing,* 4(4), 337–52.

Laws, E. and LePelley, B. (2000) 'Managing complexity and change in tourism: the case of a historic city'. *International Journal of Tourism,* 2(4), 229–46.

Laws, E. and Ryan, C. (1992) 'Service on flights: issues and analysis by use of diaries'. *Journal of Travel and Tourism Marketing*, **1**(3), 61–72.

Laws, E., Buhalis, D. and Craig-Smith, S. (1999) 'A structured bibliography of tourism books'. *Asia Pacific Journal of Tourism Research*, **3**(2), 47–63.

Laws, E., Scott, N. and Parfitt, N. (2002) 'Synergies in destination image management: a case study and conceptualisation'. *International Journal of Tourism Research*, **4**(1), 39–55.

Lawson, R. and Balakrishnan, W. (1998) 'Developing and managing brand image and brand concept strategies'. *American Marketing Association*, Winter, 121–6.

Leeds Castle Foundation (1994) *Leeds Castle*. London: Philip Wilson.

Lee, M. and Ulgado, F. (1997) 'Consumer evaluations of fast-food services: a cross national comparison'. *The Journal of Services Marketing*, **11**(1), 39–52.

Leong, J., Kim, W. and Ham, S. (2002) 'The effects of service recovery on repeat patronage'. *Journal of Quality Assurance in Hospitality and Tourism*, **3**(1/2), 69–94.

Leppard J. and Molyneux L. (1994) *Auditing Your Customer Service*. London: Routledge.

Levesque, T. J. and McDougall, G. H. G. (2000) 'Service problems and recovery strategies: an experiment'. *Canadian Journal of Administrative Sciences*, **17**(1), 20–37.

Levinson, H. (1971) *The Exceptional Executive*. Cambridge, MA: Harvard University Press.

Levitt, T. (1969) *The Marketing Mode*. New York: McGraw-Hill.

Lewis, R. C. and Booms, B. H. (1983) 'The marketing aspects of service quality', in L. Berry, L. Shostack and G. Upah (eds) *Emerging Perspectives on Services Marketing*. Chicago, IL: AMA.

Lewis, R. C. and Morris, S. V. (1987) 'The positive side of guest complaints'. *Cornell Hotel and Restaurant Administration Quarterly*, **27**, 13–15.

Locke, E. A. and Schweiger, D. M. (1979) 'Participation in decision making: one more look', in B. M. Staw (ed.) *Research in Organizational Behaviour 1*. Greenwich, CT: JAI Press.

Lockwood, A., Gummesson, E., Hubrecht, J. and Senior, M. (1992) 'Developing and maintaining a strategy for service quality', in R. Teare and M. Olsen (eds) *International Hospitality Management*. London: Pitman, 312–38.

Lockyer, K. G. and Oakland, J. S. (1981) 'How to sample success'. *Management Today*, July, 75–81.

Lovelock, C. H. (1994) *Services Marketing*. Englewood Cliffs, NJ: Prentice Hall.

Loveman, G. W. (1998) 'Employee satisfaction, customer loyalty, and financial performance: an empirical examination of the service profit chain in retail banking'. *Journal of Service Research*, **1**, 18–31.

Lyons, J. (1996) 'Getting customers to complain'. *Australian Journal of Hospitality Management*, 3(1), 37–50.

MacCannell, D. (1992) *Empty Meeting Ground: The Tourist Papers*. London: Routledge.

Mack, R., Mueller, R., Crotts, J. and Broderick, A. (2000) 'Perceptions, corrections and defections: implications for service recovery in the restaurant industry'. *Managing Service Quality*, 10(6), 339–46.

Maczak, A. (1995) *Travel in Early Modern Europe*. Cambridge: Polity Press.

Maister, D. H. (1985) 'The psychology of waiting lines', in J. A. Czepiel, M. R. Solomon and C. F. Surprenant (eds) *The Service Encounter: Managing Employee/Customer Interaction In Service Business*. Lexington, MA: Lexington Books, 113–23.

Marshall, C. (Sir) (1986) 'The airlines and their role in tourism developments in the United Kingdom'. Proceedings of *The Prospects for Tourism in Britain*, Financial Times Conferences, London, 10–15.

Masberg, B. A. and Silverman, L. H. (1996) 'Visitor experiences at heritage sites: a phenomenological approach'. *Journal of Travel Research*, 34(4), 20–5.

Mathisen, H. (1988) 'Adjusting the aircraft product to emerging customer needs'. TTRA Proceedings, 247–9.

Mattsson, L. (1985) 'An application of a network approach to marketing: defending and changing market positions', in N. Dholakia and J. Arndt (eds) *Alternative Paradigms for Widening Market Theory*. Greenwich, CT: JAI Press.

McCarthy, J. (1960) *Basic Marketing: A Management Approach*. Homewood, IL: Irwin.

McCarthy, W. and Perreault, E. J. (1988) *Essentials of Marketing*. Homewood, IL: Irwin.

McCollough, M. A., Berry, L. and Yavas, M. S. (2000) 'An empirical investigation of customer satisfaction after service failure and recovery'. *Journal of Service Research*, 3(2), 121–37.

McCracken, G. (1990) *Culture and Consumption*. Bloomington, IN: Indiana University Press.

McKenna, R (1994) *Relationship Marketing: Successful Strategies for the Age of the Customer*. Reading, MA: Addison Wesley.

Medlik, S. (1993) *Dictionary of Transport, Travel and Hospitality*. Oxford: Butterworth Heinemann.

Middleton, V. T. C. (1989) 'Marketing the margin'. *Quarterly Review of Marketing*, Winter, 14–17.

Middleton, V. T. C. (1991) *Marketing in Travel and Tourism*. Oxford: Heinemann.

Miller, J. L., Craighead, C. W. and Karwan, K. R. (2000) 'Service recovery: a framework and empirical investigation'. *Journal of Operations Management*, 18(4), 387–400.

Mok, C. and Armstrong, R. (1996) 'Sources of information used by

Hong Kong and Taiwanese leisure travellers'. *Australian Journal of Hospitality Management*, 3(1), 31–5.

Moscardo, G. (1999) *Making Visitors Mindful*. Champaign, IL: Sagamore.

Neuman, W. (1994) *Social Research Methods: Qualitative and Quantitative Approaches* (2nd edition). Needham Heights, MA: Allyn and Bacon.

Noe, F. (1999) *Tourist Service Satisfaction: Hotel, Transport and Recreation*. Champaign, IL: Sagamore.

Normann, R. (1991) *Service Management: Strategy and Leadership In Service Businesses*. Chichester: Wiley.

Nyquist, J. D., Bitner, M. J. and Booms, B. H. (1985) 'Identifying communication difficulties in the service encounter: a critical incident approach', in J. A. Czepiel, M. R. Solomon and C. F. Surprenant (eds) *The Service Encounter: Managing Employee/Customer Interaction in Service Business*. Lexington, MA: Lexington Books, 195–212.

Oliver, R. (1989) 'Processing of the satisfaction response in consumption: a suggested framework and research propositions'. *Journal of Consumer Satisfaction, Dissatisfaction and Complaining Behaviour*, 2, 1–16.

Olshavsky, R. W. (1973) 'Customer-salesman interaction in appliance retailing'. *Journal of Marketing Research*, May, 208–12.

Pan, G. and Laws, E. (2001) 'Tourism marketing opportunities for Australia in China'. *Journal of Vacation Marketing*, 8(1), 39–48.

Parasuraman, A., Zeithmal, V. A. and Berry, L. (1985) 'A conceptual model of service quality and its implications for future research'. *Journal of Marketing*, 49, 41–50.

Parasuraman, A., Zeithmal, V. A. and Berry, L. (1988) 'SERVQUAL: multiple item scale for measuring consumer perceptions of service quality'. *Journal of Retailing*, 64(1), 12–40.

Parasuraman, A., Zeithmal, V. A. and Berry, L. (1990) *A Conceptual Model of Service Quality and its Implications for Future Research*. Cambridge, MA: Marketing Service Institute.

Park, C., Whan, B., Jaworski, J. and MacInnis, D. J. (1986) 'Strategic brand concept/image management'. *Journal of Marketing*, 50, October, 135–45 (winner of the Alpha Kappa Psi Award for the article published in the *Journal of Marketing* in 1986 that best advances the practices of marketing).

Parkhe, A. (1993) 'Messy research: methodological prepositions and theory development in international joint ventures'. *Academy of Management Review*, 18(2), 491–500.

Patching, D. (1990) *Practical Soft Systems Analysis*. London: Pitman.

Payne, A. and Ballantyne, D. (1991) *Relationship Marketing: Bringing Quality, Customer Service and Marketing Together*. Oxford: Butterworth Heinemann.

Peters, T. and Austin, N. (1985) *A Passion For Excellence*. New York: Random House.

Pine II, J. and Gilmore, H. H. (1999) *The Experience Economy: Work is Theatre and Every Business a Stage*. Boston, MA: Harvard Business School Press.

Porter, M. (1985) *Competitive Advantage*. New York: The Free Press/Macmillan.

Prideaux, B. (2000) 'The role of the transport system in the growth of coastal resorts – an examination of resort development in South East Queensland'. PhD Thesis, The Department of Tourism and Leisure Management, The University of Queensland.

Prus, R. C. (1989) *Pursuing Customers: An Ethnography of Marketing Activities*. London: Sage.

Pyo, S. (ed.) (2002) *Benchmarks in Hospitality and Tourism*. Binghamton, NY: Haworth Press.

Raaij, W. (1986) 'Consumer research on tourism mental and behavioural constructs'. *Annals of Tourism Research*, **13**, 1–9.

Rafii, F. and Kampas, P. J. (2002) 'How to identify your enemies before they destroy you'. *Harvard Business Review*, November, 115–23.

Raitz, K and Dakhil, M. (1989) 'A note about information sources for preferred recreational environments'. *Journal of Travel Research*, Spring, 45–9.

Ramaswamy, R. (1996) *Design and Management of Service Processes*. Reading, MA: Addison Wesley.

Rao, A. and Hashimoto, K. (1997) 'Universal and culturally specific aspects of managerial influence: a study of Japanese managers'. *Leadership Quarterly*, 8(3), 295–312.

Rapert, M. and Wren, B. (1998) 'Service quality as a competitive opportunity'. *Journal of Services Marketing*, 12(3), 223–35.

Rathmell, J. M. (1966) 'What is meant by services?' *Journal of Marketing*, **30**(4), 32–6.

Reisenger, Y. and Waryszak, R. (1994) 'Assessment of service quality for international tourists in hotels: an exploratory study of Japanese tourists in Australia'. *Australian Journal of Hospitality Management*, 1(2), 11–15.

Relihan III, W. (1989) 'The yield management approach to hotel pricing'. *Cornell Hotel and Restaurant Administration*, 30(1), 40–5.

Robinson, S. (1999) 'Measuring service quality, current thinking and future requirements'. *Marketing Intelligence and Planning*, 7(1), 21–32.

Robledo, M. A. (2001) 'Measuring and managing service quality: integrating customer expectations'. *Managing Service Quality*, 11(1), 22–31.

Ross, G. F. (1993) 'Service quality and management: the perceptions of hospitality employees'. *Journal of Tourism Studies*, 4(2), 55–68.

Rust, R., Zahorik, A. and Keiningham, T. (1995) *Service Marketing.* New York: HarperCollins.

Ryan, C. (1991) *Recreational Tourism: A Social Science Perspective.* London: Routledge.

Ryan, C. (1995) *Researching Tourist Satisfaction.* London: Routledge.

Sainsbury, R. (1990) 'Concepts without boundaries'. Inaugural Professional Lecture, Kings College, London.

Saleh, F. and Ryan, C. (1992) 'Conviviality: a source of satisfaction for hotel guests? An application of the SERVQUAL model', in P. Johnson and B. Thomas (eds) *Choice and Demand in Tourism.* London: Mansell, 107–22.

Sasser, E. W., Olsen, P. R. and Wycoff, D. D. (1978) *Management Of Service Operations.* Boston, MA: Allyn and Bacon.

Saxby, C. L., Tat, P. K. and Thompson Johansen, J. (2000) 'Measuring consumer perceptions of procedural justice in a complaint context'. *The Journal of Consumer Affairs*, **34**(2), 204–16.

Scherl, L. M. and Smithson, M. A. (1987) 'New dimension to content analysis: exploring relationships amongst thematic categories'. *Quality and Quantity*, **21**, 199–208.

Schmenner, R. (1995) *Service Operations Management.* Englewood Cliffs, NJ: Prentice Hall.

Senior, M. and Akehurst, G. (1992) 'The perceptual service blueprinting paradigm'. *Proceedings of the Second QUIS Conference*, St Johns University, New York, 177–92.

Shemwell, D. and Cronin, J. J. (1994) 'Services marketing strategies for coping with demand/supply imbalance'. *Journal of Services Marketing*, **8**(4), 14–24.

Shepherd, C. D. (1999) 'Service quality and the sales force: a tool for competitive advantage'. *Journal of Personal Selling and Sales Management*, **XIX**(3), 77–82.

Shewart, W. A. (1931) *Economic Control of Quality in Manufactured Products.* New York: Van Nostrand.

Shin, S. (1994) *The Logic Status of Diagrams.* Cambridge: Cambridge University Press.

Shostack, L. (1981) 'How to design a service', in J. H. Donnelley and W. R. George (eds) *Marketing of Services.* New York: AMA.

Shostack, L. (1984) 'Designing services that deliver'. *Harvard Business Review*, **62**, January–February, 133–9.

Shostack, L. (1985) 'Planning the service encounter', in J. A. Czepiel, M. R. Solomon and C. F. Surprenant (eds) *The Service Encounter: Managing Employee/Customer Interaction In Service Business.* Lexington, MA: Lexington Books, 243–53.

Shostack, L. (1987) 'Service positioning through structural change'. *Journal of Marketing*, **51**, January, 34–43.

Shostack, L. and Kingman-Brundage, J. (1991) 'How to design a service', in C. Congram and L. Friedman (eds) *The AMA Handbook of Marketing For Service Industries*. New York: AMA, 24–61.

Siha, S. (1999) 'A classified model for applying the theory of constraints to service organizations'. *Managing Service Quality*, **9**(4), 255–65.

Solomon, M. R., Surprenant, C., Czepiel, J. A. and Gutman, E. G. (1982) *Service Encounters as Dyadic Interactions: A Role Theory Perspective*. Working Paper 82, New York University.

Soutar, G. N. (2001) 'Service quality, customer satisfaction, and value: an examination of their relationships', in J. Kandampully, C. Mok and B. Spark (eds) *Service Quality Management in Hospitality, Tourism and Leisure*. New York: The Hayworth Hospitality Press, 97–110.

Sparks, B. (2002) 'I would have felt better if only . . . or, how to enhance customer satisfaction following service problems'. *Journal of Quality Assurance in Hospitality and Tourism*, **3**(1/2), 53–68.

Spies, K., Hesse, F. and Loesch, K. (1997) 'Store atmosphere, mood and purchasing behaviour'. *International Journal of Research in Marketing*, **14**(9), 1–17.

Spreng, R., Gilbert, D. and Mackoy, R. (1995) 'Service recovery: impact on satisfaction and intentions'. *Journal of Services Marketing*, **9**(1), 15–23.

Standards Australia (1990) *Quality Management and Quality System Elements. Part 2: Guidelines to Services*. Homebush, NSW: The Standards Association of Australia.

Stafford, J. E. (1966) 'Effects of group influence on consumer brand preference'. *Journal of Marketing Research*, **3**, 68–75.

Stauss, B. (1993) 'Using the critical incident technique in measuring and managing service quality', in E. Scheuing and W. Christopher (eds) *The Service Quality Handbook*. New York: American Marketing Institute, 408–27.

Stauss, B. (2002) 'The dimensions of complaint satisfaction: process and outcome complaint satisfaction versus cold fact and warm act complaint satisfaction'. *Managing Service Quality*, **12**(3), 173–83.

Sternlicht, B. (2002) 'Hotels pay back'. *Business Traveler*, November, 16.

Stevens, P., Knutson, B. and Patton, M. (1995) 'DINESERV: a tool for measuring service quality in restaurants'. *The Cornell Hotel and Restaurant Administration Quarterly*, **36**(2), 56–9.

Swan, J. and Bowers, M. (1998) 'Services quality and satisfaction: the process of people doing things together'. *Journal of Services Marketing*, **12**(1), 59–72.

Swarbrooke, J. (2001) 'Distribution channels: ethics and sustainability', in D. Buhalis and E. Laws (eds) *Tourism Distribution Channels: Practices, Issues and Transformations*. London: Continuum, 87–102.

Szybillo, G. J. and Jacoby, J. (1974) 'Intrinsic versus extrinsic cues as determinants of perceived product quality'. *Journal of Applied Psychology*, **59**, 74–7.

Tan, K. C. and. Pawitra, T. A. (2001) 'Integrating SERVQUAL and Kano's model into QFD for service excellence development'. *Managing Service Quality*, **11**(6) 418–30.

TARP (1979) *Consumer Complaint Handling in America: Final Report.* Washington, DC: Office of Consumer Affairs.

Tax, S., Brown, S. W. and Chandrashekaran, M. (1998) 'Customer evaluation of service complaint experiences: implications for relationship marketing'. *Journal of Marketing*, **62**(2), 60–76.

Teas, K. (1994) 'Expectations as a comparison of standards in measuring service quality: an assessment and reassessment'. *Journal of Marketing*, **58**(1), 132–9.

Teye, V. and Leclerc, D. (1998) 'Product and service delivery satisfaction among North American cruise passengers'. *Tourism Management*, **19**(2), 153–60.

Thomas, M. (1987) 'Coming to terms with the customer'. *Personnel Management*, February, 24–28.

Toffler, A. (1980) *The Third Wave*. London: Pan Books.

Tolman, E. (1932) *Purposive Behaviour in Animals and Men*. New York: Appleton Century.

Trent, R. and Monczka, R. (1999) 'Achieving world-class supplier quality'. *Total Quality Management*, **10**(6), 927–38.

Tribe, J. (2002) 'Mystery shopping: theory and practice', in E. Laws (ed.) *Tourism Marketing: Quality and Service Management Perspectives*. London: Continuum, 75–86.

Tribe, J. and Snaith, T. (1998) 'From SERVQUAL to HOLSAT: holiday satisfaction in Varadero, Cuba'. *Tourism Management*, **19**(1), 25–34.

Tung, W., Capella, L. and Tat, P. (1997) 'Service pricing: a multistep synthetic approach'. *Journal of Services Marketing*, **11**(1), 53–65.

Upah, G. D. and Fulton, J. W. (1985) 'Situation creation in service marketing', in J. A. Czepiel, M. R. Solomon and C. F. Surprenant (eds) *The Service Encounter: Managing Employee/Customer Interaction In Service Business*. Lexington, MA: Lexington Books, 255–63.

Urry, J. (1990) *The Tourist Gaze*. London: Sage.

van der Wiele, T., Boselie, P. and Hesselink, M. (2002) 'Empirical evidence for the relationship between customer satisfaction and business performance'. *Managing Service Quality*, **12**(3), 184–93.

Varca, P. (1999) 'Work stress and customer service delivery'. *Journal of Services Marketing*, **13**(3), 229–41.

Vellas, F. and Becherel, L. (1995) *International Tourism: An Economic Perspective*. London: Macmillan Business.

Vine, D. and Hele, J. (1998) 'Less paperwork with the new ISO 9000'. *Qualityworld'*, August, 32–3.

Walle, A. H. (1997) 'Quantitative versus qualitative tourism research'. *Annals of Tourism Research*, **24**(3), 524–36.

Wang Ruixue (1991) 'AngloChinese understanding on the tourist trail'. *China Now*, 1(39), 8–9.

Weitz, B. A. (1981) 'Effective sales interactions: a contingency framework'. *Journal of Marketing*, 45, 185–95.

Wilkie, W. L. (1986) *Consumer Behaviour*. New York: Wiley.

Williams, R. and Visser, R. (2002) 'Customer satisfaction: it is dead but it will not lie down'. *Managing Service Quality*, 12(3), 194–200.

Winsted, K. F. (1997) 'The service experience on two cultures: a behavioural perspective'. *Journal of Retailing*, 73(3), 337–60.

Wisner, J. (1999) 'A study of successful quality improvement programs in the transportation industry'. *Benchmarking: An International Journal*, 6(2), 147–63.

World Tourism Organization (WTO) (2002) *Compendium of Tourism Statistics*. Madrid: World Tourism Organization.

Yasin, M. M. and Yavas, U. (1999) 'Enhancing customer orientation of service delivery systems: an integrative framework'. *Managing Service Quality*, 9(3), 198–203.

Yin, R. K. (1994) *Case Study Research: Design and Methods*. London: Sage.

Zaleznik, A. (1977) 'Managers and leaders: are they different?' *Harvard Business Review*, 55(3), 67–78.

Zeithmal, V. A. (2000) 'Service quality, profitability, and the economic worth of customers: what we know and what we need to learn'. *Journal of Academy of Marketing Science*, 28(1), 67–85.

Zeithmal, V. A., Berry, L. and Parasuraman, A. (1988) 'Communication and control processes in the delivery of service quality'. *Journal of Marketing*, 52, April, 35–48.

Zeithmal, V. A., Berry, L. and Parasuraman, A. (1996) 'The behavioural consequences of service quality'. *Journal of Marketing*, 60, 31–46.

Zeithmal, V. A., Parasuraman, A. and Berry, L. (1985) 'Problems and strategies in services marketing'. *Journal of Marketing*, 49, Spring, 33–46.

Zeithmal, V. A., Parasuraman, A. and Berry, L. (1990) *Delivering Quality Service*. New York: The Free Press/Macmillan.

Zemke, R. and Schaaf, D. (1989) *The Service Edge*. New York: Penguin.

Index

Acid test, 34–36, 128
Advertising, 3, 112–123, 128
Approach–avoidance continuum, 53
Augmented service, 104–106, 105, 122
Automated service, 21

Barriers to market entry, 104
Benchmark, 168
Blueprinting, xvii, 57–78, 91–98, 142, 167–169, 173
Brand, 9, 108–109
British Airways, 5, 53, 163–167

Case study method, xv, 6, 28–30
China, 1, 56–57
Choice and risk, 2, 101–102, 118, 123, 125
Commoditization, 116
Competition, 2, 104, 106, 108, 115, 119, 132, 136
Complaints, 90, 121, 147–148, 151–158
Complexity theory, 3, 30–31
  of tourism system, xvi, 9, 91, 119, 133–136, 158, 173–175
Concorde, 52, 104, 127
Consistent quality, 10, 15, 107–108, 131, 159
Consumer perception, 9, 72–73, 82–85, 125–126, 176
  consumer self image, 112
  purchasing decisions, 2

Consumer rights, 3, 101
  experience, 14, 20–21, 32, 80–85, 131
Consumerist gap, 25, 32–36, 40, 78, 84, 90, 93, 112, 141, 150–155
  method, 38–46
  taxonomy, 38–39.
Content analysis, 41–42, 151–155
Continuous service improvement, 10, 29–30, 105, 146, 176
Core service, 62, 103–106, 125–126, 149
Cost of service quality, 91, 155–156
Critical incident technique, 42–43, 151–155
Customer empowerment, 139, 140
Customer focus, xviii, 129
Customer loyalty, 14, 122–123, 148, 156

Destination improvement, 53, 112
Diagrams, 14
Diary method, 40, 93–96
Dissatisfaction, 35, 90–91
Dynamics of tourism service development, xviii, 2, 9, 29, 112, 134–135
Dysfunctional customer behaviour, 132

Empathy, 132
Empowerment, 139, 142–143, 147

Exit, 141
Expectations, 26, 43–44, 73, 83,
  134–135, 112, 176
External marketing, 171

Failpoints, 1, 4–5, 38, 55–56, 70–71,
  90–91, 148–155
  recovery, 55–56, 84, 90,
    149–155
Feedback, 15, 25
Fuzzy categories, 11

Garvin, 79, 107, 159
Government regulations, 3, 49–51,
  163
Gronroos, 15, 17, 20, 80–81, 84,
  100, 108, 129
Gummesson, 11, 28, 82, 133, 136,
  140, 145, 158, 171, 173

Hard and soft service elements, 27,
  48, 83
High and low contact service design,
  63–72 139

Image, 9, 20
Information, 101, 128
Innovation, 3, 105–108
Inseparability, 17, 135
Intangibility, 16
Interdependency of tourism industry,
  xviii, 26, 107, 158, 159,
  170–173
Internal marketing, 129
Investment in tourism infrastructure,
  xv, 2
Involvement theory, 123–126
ISO 9000, xviii, 143–144
IT (information technology), 176

JND (just noticeable difference),
  40–41, 141

Lifestyle segmentation, 3, 20
Line of visibility, 58–60

Management myopia, 20–21
Management responsibilities, 96,
  162–167
  limits, 173–176
Mapping, *see blueprinting*
Market research, 53, 105
Marketing paradigm, 101
Marketing, 100–129, 138
Messy problems, 27
Moments of Truth, 21, 43
  see also Service encounter

Operational characteristics of services,
  14, 16–17
Organizational change, 73–77
  climate, 162–170
  pyramid, 160–162

Part encounter, 38
Part time marketers, 133
Participant observations, 40
Perishability, 18–19
Positioning, 29, 52, 109–122
Power differential, 134
Price, 115–121
  and quality, 120–121
Problem or crisis, 146–156
Productivity, 130
Profit impact of quality management,
  15, 91, 145–146, 155–156
Purchase decision, 100–129

Qualitative research, 28
Quality, 79–99, 141
  audit, 144–145
  dimensions, 80–81
  research, 10–11, 79–85, 93,
    142, 177

Reference price, 120
Relationship marketing, 171
Research, 9–11, 19–20, 22–29,
  32–47, 86, 89, 176
  1st and 2nd generation, 30,
    158–160

Risk, 102, 118, 129
Role theory, 13, 27, 138

Satisfaction and quality, xv, 1, 14,
    36–37, 79–99, 135
Self image, 112
Service bundles, 106–108
    design, 46–48
    differentiation, 108–109
    errors, 55–56
    events, 33–38, 134
    gaps, 85–88, 113
    organizational culture, 167–169
    performance criteria, 14, 54
    phases, 14–22, 61, 131
    specifications, 49–54, 131
    standards, 2, 10, 29–30,
        141–146, 159
    see also Failpoints
Service encounter, xvii, 10, 22, 38,
    92, 135–140, 142, 230
    cultural factors, 176
    job satisfaction, 132
    power differential, 134
Services contrasted to manufacturing,
    10, 13, 16–19, 31, 81, 158
SERVQUAL, xviii, 36, 85–89, 176
Servuction, 139, 140
Sheraton, 108
    Sheraton promise, 5
Shostack, 4–6, 9, 57, 161, 135, 139,
    162

Stakeholders, xv, xvii, 15, 112–115,
    176
Stress, 62, 132, 134, 140
Style, 50–51, 104
Systems theory, 22–28

Team work, 159–160
Terrorism, 1, 21
Time in modelling services, 58–60,
    76, 126–129, 134, 148, 173
Tourism, definition, 32
Trading up, 103
Type A&B service elements, 13, 27,
    38, 48, 51, 85, 136,
    140, 150

Uncertainty, 99, 118, 131

Variation in satisfaction, 15,
    123–126, 152–155, 159
Vegetarian meal service, 43–45
Voice, 141

WOM (word of mouth), 5, 14, 91,
    101, 148, 156
WTO, 1

Zone of visibility, 64–65

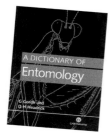
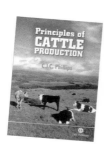